Zen Starter Pack:

2 books in 1:

Meditation for Beginners and Buddhism for Beginners - Premium Bundle to Master Transcendental Meditation basics, Zen and Buddhism from Zero with Practical Applications

CONTENTS

BUDDHISM FOR BEGINNERS

MEDITATION FOR BEGINNERS

BUDDHISM FOR BEGINNERS:

The incredible book that will definitively change your perspective on Buddhism and Zen Meditation

by

Gregory F. George

Introduction to meditation

Zen says "When I'm hungry, I eat. When I'm tired, I sleep". But you have to do it conscientiously, without getting carried away by the events. Zen is a daily consciousness, as Matsu said.[1]

Without getting carried away by events. A phrase by Fabrizio De Andrè comes into my mind: "Continuerai a farti scegliere o finalmente sceglierai?"[2](Will you continue to make you choose, or will you finally choose?)

I will often make analogies between the two cultures, not only to show differences and similarities, but to show what's missing in our actions to be Zen.

You will find many pop references. Both because of what I've just written, and to make your reading more enjoyable. You will also find not really pop references, because they are part of my cultural background and in this book you'll find also personal experiences. I decided to write them because I think some of life lived notes and anecdotes can make reading more enjoyable. And also because it is thanks to my experience and my cultural background that I've been able to write this book, and it is through your experience and your cultural baggage that you will understand it and approach Zen. In conclusion you will also find a few tales.

There will also be references to Greek philosophy. Listen to the words of Robert M. Piercing [3]

"In this book there is a lot of talk about the way of seeing things typical of the ancient Greeks."[4]. Well, I am not the first to combine Zen and Philosophy. This *auctoritas* comforts me.

Part 1

Definitions, questions and answers

Let's begin by trying to contextualize Zen, and to give it a smattering to those who do not know anything about it.

What is Zen? The monk and Socrates

One does not learn to play the organ from those who build the organs, but from those who play them.

[Galileo Galilei]

What is Zen? What are its doctrinal principles? It is easy to answer the first question. It is a meditation practice that comes from the Buddhist religion, indeed, it is within the Buddhist religion. It is less easy to answer the second question. In fact, it has no doctrine in a metaphysical and transcendent sense, and refers to those of Buddhism. It has rules and practices that have only one purpose: happiness here and now. Not only in the sense that it does not give importance to paradisiacal comforting ideas of a life after death, but also in that which doesn't think too much about the future. Here and now, but right here and now, in this instant and in this place. With the advantage that this action made *hic et nunc*, we will benefit for a long time. Another very important thing is that we can make practically all the actions of our day, or at least a good part, zen. All things will shine with a new light. In some cases, they will just start to shine, from opaque they were.

Zen must be practiced, not understood. Perhaps it is for this reason that for us Westerners, at least at the beginning, may seem difficult. Socrates used to walk around the streets of Athens asking "what is it?" He was looking for the essence, not for descriptions. He proudly defined himself as the gadfly. He was a little annoying, according to what he got there. A Buddhist monk would have answered him with silence, and make him do Zen practices, explaining them. Moreover, when the monks meditate, they must also bear insects.

When Zen was born?

According to the Treccani Encyclopedia, between the Twelfth and the Thirteenth Century.[5] But the situation is not so simple: here's what the Zen Rome website reports:

Zen, which literally means meditation, has ancient origins dating back 5,000 years. Practiced in the pre-Aryan civilization in India, it was rediscovered by the Buddha as a vehicle to access a dimension of wisdom and spirituality.[6]

So, in practice?

For this reason, the Chinese tradition of Chán is also sometimes called *Zen*, but also the *Sòn* Korean and *Thiền* Vietnamese traditions. "*Zen* points directly to the human mind-heart, look at your true Nature and become Buddha."

The Bodhidharma definition of Zen:

A special transmission outside the scriptures
No dependence upon words and letters
Direct pointing at the soul of man
Seeing into one's nature and the entertainment of Buddhahood.

(*Four Sacred Verses of Bodhidharma*)

Who was Bodhidharma[7]

He was a Persian Buddhist monk who lived between the 5th and 6th centuries AD. According to tradition, he was the twenty-eighth heir to an unbroken line of descending directives from the Buddha..[8]

Who can practice Zen?

Zen is not an abstruse thing for Buddhist monks and weird Westerners, as we can all be Zen. It is not necessary to be Buddhists or fanatical of the East. I certainly am neither one nor the other, yet every day I find a way to do Zen practices because I like them and doing that makes me feel good. Moreover, a practice that is so little conceptual, can only be within everyone's reach. Therefore, whether you are an atheist, a Catholic, a Buddhist, etc., do it without hesitation. If you don't believe me, read here.

It is possible to show in a well-founded way, that the Zen exercise does not distance the exerciser from Christ, as feared by someone, but makes him find the way to be in him, a way to concretely experience the binomial "Christ-in-me "And" I-in-Christ. [...]Those who participate in the Zen exercises, or what is proposed in Europe under this name or other similar ones, are generally people who come from the "Western" cultural sphere. They can be Christians more or less deeply inserted into their religious beliefs; or non-baptized people who are looking for a religious point of view. The reaction to these exercises is different, and depends on the origin of each one. Simply rejecting the Zen exercise is totally inappropriate, as well as considering it dangerous and always warning against it. Not every medicine helps and helps everyone.[9]

In short, Zen does not nail you up and does not claim exclusivity.

As for your lifestyle, you certainly won't have to upset it. Once the meditation is over, you will return to normal, but Zen will have a very positive influence on your daily routine [10]. So much, that you probably won't find it monotonous anymore.[11]

What is the etymology of the word Zen?

The word Zen derives from the Japanese pronunciation of a Chinese character, that in Middle Chinese is pronounced dʑiɛn. According to other hypotheses, instead, Zen derives from the Korean Seon, which derives from the Chinese Chan, which derives from the pali Dhana which indicates the practice of meditation.

I was undecided whether to insert this part or not. The thing that matters most to me, is that you can grasp the essence of Zen, and learn to practice it by gaining concrete advantages in your everyday life. Never mind if you don't know, or don't remember the etymology or the history of Zen, at least from the point of view of this book.

Because even those who have not read Freud can live a hundred years, as Rino Gaetano sings in "Mio fratello è figlio unico". If you want to live well, the most important thing is that you live in a Zen way.

Are there several Zen schools, or just one?

There are three of them and they are called Obaku, Rinzai and Soto.

The Rizai is more austere and therefore it became the favorite of the Samurai.[12]

What do the different Zen schools have in common?

First of all, the zazen, which is the meditation practice. Then, the fact of giving less attention to the study of sutras. Thirdly, the attention to detail when it comes to the transmission of the "lineage".

What is a sutra?

In Brahmanism, a sutra is a sacred text that transmits a teaching. In Buddhism, the sutras are the Buddha's sermons collected by the disciples after his death. Sutra is a Sanskrit term and means wire.[13]

What is the purpose of Zen?

The purpose of Zen is awareness. Awareness of what? Awareness that we do not coincide with our thoughts. Awareness that almost everything we have is not necessary. Awareness that our "I" is illusory, because, like all phenomena, it is transient and apparent. A Zen story speaks of cookies of different shapes, but all cut from the same cloth.

We must not escape from bad things, because we must learn to deal even with the negative and difficult components of life. Zen wants to teach us that even negative episodes can be useful, and if we can learn from them, they will strengthen us.

Who makes zen does not perform miracles, but manages to fully live the present moment despite all adversities.

What is the main obstacle?

The main obstacle is our ego.

*In order to know oneself, first of all it is important to separate what we are from our **ego**, that is the **false identity** that practically every person has developed* *by growing up. Our mind is continually dominated by endless thoughts of **self-centeredness**, greed, attachment, anger, pride, envy, etc.*

The ego is always lurking, and it is the cause of most suffering, as well as food for the monkey mind. It is essential to be aware of his presence to understand that you are not your thoughts.[14]

How do we reach awareness?

Through meditation.

What can't Zen do?

Zen cannot make suffering disappear, but it helps us to accept it. Awareness also concerns the negative things in life and, above all, suffering. Zen helps us to accept it. Attention: not to resign ourselves, but to set our life based on them. Suffering can help us shed light on our relationships with others. Attention bis: it is useless to remove it, because sooner or later it comes back, but it is not that we have to look for it. We must accept suffering without feeling guilty and without accusing anyone. We must accept suffering knowing that life is loved despite the things that make us feel bad. We must accept suffering, knowing that we are not suffering even if it is part of us. We must help those who are suffering, and try to soothe everyone's pain.

Furthermore, Zen does not make us have mystical or extrasensory visions. But it can make us have insight, which is an immediate restructuring of the understanding of reality. It does not derive from a series of arguments, but, indeed, from an intuition. An example of insight is that of Newton's apple.

What is the difference between detachment and non-attachment?

Detachment indicates a desire not to have, or not to do something. Non-attachment means letting things happen and reaching us, without fretting us too much in case of loss (so let's enjoy them!). Zen supports non-attachment.

In short, we can also live without them. In the face of any objection, we clarify that no one, not even Zen, takes theft or loss of money lightly. But the point is that according to Zen, our happiness should not depend on them.

Similarly, for the desire to have new goods. A Mass is sung "Search first the Kingdom of God and his justice and all the rest will be given to you more". The Zen states "seek the richness that is within you, and welcome all the remaining pleasurable things that will come to you". I remember a version of Latin that spoke of a city on fire, destroyed/at the mercy of enemies and one [15] that replied "omnia mecum porto" (I take all my belongings with me, that is to say my wisdom and my culture) to those who were surprised to see it peaceful and calm despite the huge losses. Don't you find it a little Zen?

Seneca spoke of the firmness of the essay that remains unperturbed at external events, because it draws from within itself its own strength and awareness of its own value.

He was a little zen too. Moreover, every wise person who is aware of his own value has a hint of Zen in him or better, he shares some values of Zen without being aware of it.

Why does Zen seem difficult?

Probably, because it has no intellectual or cognitive approach.[16] The Japanese use the expression "I shin den shin", which we could translate as "from heart to heart". Zen masters do not explain, Zen masters show. We are referring to all activities related to Zen. And when they show, the disciples cannot ask questions.[17] The disciple learns by looking for years at what the teacher is doing, especially in gestures. All this must take place in silence.

Part 2

Meditation

There are different types of meditation. We will only see a few. All of them have an element in common and it is breathing.[18]

Cross-legged meditation and other types of meditation

The legs take the so-called position of the lotus, while the closed eyes serve to meet the frequency of 8-13 hertz, which is the alpha rhythm, that is the rhythm that allows us to disconnect from the external world, easily reachable by a non-stressed person.[19]

The position one assumes when one sits down to meditate is called zazen.[20]

The term *zazen* indicates precisely the posture of the Buddha.[21]

We must keep our eyes closed or half-closed to prevent the mind from being distracted by the outside world. The mind looks a bit like a monkey, it is a phrase that often occurs in the Zen world.

Koan Meditation

One type of meditation is called koan. Yes part by breathing three times, and it is best to do it using your belly. We inhale deeply and breathe out slowly and prolongedly. While we do it, we count from one to ten. Each breath corresponds to a number. It must be done ten times, from one to ten. If we distract ourselves, we must start from one. Koan meditation is one of the first things that Zen monks face, but it is also useful for the laity as it develops firmness and stability, two determining elements when making a decision. Furthermore, it helps us to maintain concentration.

Koan meditation uses koans, which are paradoxes.[22]

Shikantaza meditation has its clear rules. It is practiced by monks all over the world, and we can do it ourselves. The word shi means to cease, but we can translate it with tranquility, stillness. The word Kan we can translate it with awareness.[23] Taza indicates sitting in the simplicity of life.

Shikantaza meditation should be done in silence by contemplating external phenomena (but not their visual image), without interfering with them. We must not only be silent, but stop thoughts. We observe things and events and we keep the ego at bay. Let's go to shikantaza meditation in the most peaceful place possible, with the right light, with the right temperature, away from unpleasant odors, and maybe with some essence. In short, nothing should disturb us. Don't do it when we're tired and when we're weighed down.

The ideal would be to sit on a round cushion, the so-called zafu, placed on a blanket, and turn against the wall in order to have as few distractions as possible.

In theory we should put ourselves in the lotus position, but crossing our legs will suffice. The eyes must be half-open and set a point below us by about forty-five degrees. Better not to keep them closed completely, to avoid the risk of falling asleep. Let's take a first breath by sucking in very deep, and bring it to the abdomen. After that, let's exhale involving the pelvis and the whole lower part. In this way we are laying the foundations of our meditation. Let's repeat it three times. Let's move on to the second type of breath type. Also in this case, inspiring we will bring the breath to the abdomen, but exhaling we will expand the breath in the central part of the body. We do it to open the bust, to straighten the back, to relax energy and emotions. Let's do it twice. The third way of breathing is that the exhalation takes place in the upper part of the body, but also in the whole body, in order to feel ourselves totally present. All this will give us calm and stability.

Breathing must be abdominal, and must be done with the mouth closed, with the nostrils, calmly and silently. We do not force the rhythm of breathing, but let it flow naturally. We should hardly think we're breathing. Let thoughts flow freely, without suppressing or suffocating them, but neither without trying to capture them or understand them. In short, let's not give it too much importance. The same is true for sensations, both for positive and negative ones: let us accept them and not reject them. If they are positive, let's enjoy them but don't stick to them.

Shikantaza breathing must last at least a quarter of an hour / twenty minutes, but it is not forbidden to last even all evening. After all, we just have to sit and do nothing, in silence.

Thanks to shikantaza we will rediscover the awareness of our unity with the rest of the Universe. A unity that has always existed and for which we only needed to become aware.

No one forces us to meditate, and we can stop doing it whenever we want.

After the shikantaza meditation the four vows can be recited like the Zen monks do.[24]

The Pebble Meditation

It is simple and can be done by everyone, even by children. Indeed, it can be a fun way to introduce them to meditation. It can be done either alone or in company. They take pebbles and put them next to each other. He takes one in his hand and meditates on a sentence, breathing adequately.[25]

Other types of meditation

A new day[26]

Let's start right from the beginning, that is to say from awakening. Buddhist monks wake up when it is still dark, and enter the new day with the sun. But we don't need that much, of course. On the other hand, we can do a Zen meditation since awakening.

The same awakening can set us well towards meditation, being almost propaedeutic. It is recommended that it be done with a sweet and harmonious sound. It is also advised not to postpone waking up with the timeless "five more minutes" and if we really can't do without it when we decide that it's time to officially wake up let's do it with the right attitude and above all in a correct way. Certainly, a correct way is Zen. That will please even the laziest because it does not force us to get out of bed too abruptly and suddenly.

Yes part with breathing. We will do meditation while breathing. First we will direct the meditation towards the neck. The neck is important because it supports the head, the seat of the mind. We will then move on to the back, abdomen, pelvis, legs and finally feet, each with its own role and importance in our lives.

Remember we talked about Kill Bill's bride? I would like to imagine that his moving feet are just one of the last moments of a correct awakening, but then I remember that the journey to the East and the learning of the techniques are later, and could not have been otherwise. However, even so we see the centrality of this part of our body.

At this point we open our eyes, observe the environment that surrounds us and let it enter the world with us on this new day.

Every day, for Zen it can be the day. A special day full of surprises and opportunities. Even before knowing Zen, I started the day with the motivational phrase: I don't know what will happen to me today. It's not so strange that I have approached this practice, right?

It is not certain that the day reserves only for us beautiful things, and to face this risk I have adopted another mantra that recites: anything goes. Even negative experiences can be useful again, if only in terms of growth. Admitted then that they are really negative, and that in the long run they do not prove to be, on the contrary, the condition of moments of possibility.

Thanks to breathing and these two mantras I can now start the day full of energy. Actually, I need other things to start loading, but let's say I'm already well prepared. The first is the physical contact of the feet (still them!) With the floor, the domestic symbol of the mother earth. My floor is cold. A cold of tiles. If yours is warm, because having the carpet or the parquet, it's ok anyway.

At this point, the ablutions. It is not just a hygienic question, but a need to feel the water running over you, to wake up and to relax.

Now, breakfast. The beauty of Zen is that it tells us to eat what we like, without too many healthy moralisms. But he tells us what to do. Indeed, above all what not to do. We don't have to look at the phone or tablet, read the news in the newspaper (options especially suitable for those who have breakfast in the bar), turn on the television or radio, don't plan the day. Let us dedicate ourselves to ourselves and those dear to us who are close to us. In particular, we become aware that a new day is beginning, and that starting with us, dear reader, my day is also your day. And we can both do a lot to make an impact. Over time, the mantra: I don't know what will happen to me today it's becoming I don't know today what I'll have the chance to do. Do you understand the difference? From suffering, to acting. A real change of mentality. Almost a Copernican revolution.

Now we will dress (it goes without saying that if we had breakfast at the bar, we dressed first). Let's not do it at random, but we carefully choose clothes and above all, colors because they express something about us and above all condition our mood. An even more important thing is the vow to be kind, sincere, benevolent, altruistic. Personally, I'm not a fan of sincerity at all costs, if you risk hurting a person with it or if it can cause problems. Better silence or even better not to say what we think. We don't have to express ourselves over everything.

Before getting dressed or just leaving the house, (re) brush your teeth. I try to do it twice every morning and while we do it we pay attention not to waste too much water, just like every time we use it

So, we woke up, we got out of bed, we washed, we had breakfast and we got dressed. Nothing strange compared to the usual. Only we did it with a different approach, dedicating more time to ourselves and our loved ones. Above all, with the desire to ensure that the usual routine leaves room for a day in which we will do everything to be happy, to be serene, to realize ourselves, to make it unique and unforgettable.

A tip: let's not get up early. Rather we reflect that by doing so we will be able to take advantage of it. I, for example, slowly carbide, so the sooner I wake up, the more awake I am (cum grano salis).[27]

Sometimes, in contrast to the ritual, I drink a coffee before meditation.

To walk

Yeah, c'mon bro, I don't wanna meditate. I hate sitting cross-legged.

Ok, maybe it was a little too much, but it is true that many find excuses. Here, I will reveal something shocking to you: to meditate, you don't need to sit with your legs crossed. Indeed, it is not really necessary to sit: you can do it even while walking. The important thing is that you walk slowly, inhaling and exhaling well. In this way, the world will become almost part of you and will be more benevolent. Thanks to the inspiration the world becomes part of us, thanks to the exhalation we return it 'digested', by now familiar.

I will tell you more: not only will you notice many more details and many elements that you did not notice before, but memories will emerge related to the place where you are doing your meditative walk. The place will become so familiar to you, that after a while you will proceed like a lion in the middle of the savannah.

It doesn't matter that this happens on the seashore, in a path, or in the center of a metropolis. The important thing is that you breathe and listen to your breath. Another very important factor is that one has to walk for the sake of walking and not to reach a goal. And if we decide to meditate while we go somewhere, we need to act like we're not going anywhere.

Thanks to it, in fact, we will be able to calm the nerves and relax. If we are in a city different from ours, it is a way to make friends with it.

One of my first meditations focused on walking. Of course, we started sitting cross-legged. To tell the truth, they made us put in the most comfortable position, then they made us walk, even with our eyes closed, asking us to pay great attention to our steps. Today I try as soon as I can to do itinerant meditation and it also helps me a lot in practical activities, for example when I have a work appointment. Also, I notice the details even when I'm in a hurry, let alone when I meditate.

For Zen it is preferable that we start doing things with the left foot because the heart is on the left. But immediately after that the right one must come, that of rationality. In short, they support each other and we need both components. The movement must start from the pelvis and at the beginning we must pay attention to the legs, after a short time the rest of the body will also "start talking to us". Meditation starts from the body and then passes into our inner part. Some Zen books refer to spirit and heart, but the first word has religious implications, and as for the heart, it is known that it is somewhat overrated. Our stomach feels the emotions, not the heart. But it usually said so, and therefore we accept it. Let's keep on with the conversation, and even our walk. Breathing. What we have to do during the walk must be done calmly, and it must start only when we are well aware that we are walking.

Also in this chapter we have seen how it is possible to transform a simple daily action carried out practically by everyone into an occasion of meditation and inner growth and search for harmony with the world. In other words, in a Zen experience. Because it is true that we take four steps to relax, but with Zen there is a qualitative leap that is given by meditation and awareness.

In the kitchen

How amazing is to eat, and how also to cook (at least for me)! And how nice to eat and cook in a zen way! We have seen before that Zen leaves people free to eat what they want and if you eat chocolate brioche every morning and sometimes French fries will not be the end of the world, but it is true that it prefers a cuisine based on herbal ingredients. and fish. Above all, it prefers seasonal ingredients. Even more important is the approach to food, both in terms of preparation and consumption.

When we are preparing our meal, let's try to be in tune with food, to treat it gently, to understand how it can be cooked at the best. Some even talk to him and listen to him, a bit like the character of Maurizio Crozza[28]. It may seem a bit of an exaggeration, but it is true that an ingredient can speak to us in its own way to suggest us, based on taste, color, texture or perfume, the way of being prepared and the combinations (each dish, according to Zen, it must contain a sweet, a salty, a spicy, a bitter and an acid part, and we find this idea also in other oriental cuisines, including the Middle Eastern one). Let us remember that we eat almost exclusively what was alive and that in a sense we make it part of ourselves by ingesting it. Anaxagoras said that everything is in everything, and that it is thanks to food that hair, nails, etc. grow, as if they were already there. Freud, on the other hand, lets us know that cannibals eat their enemies to take their strength and their virtues. It is also very important that you cook with love and dedication, so that these feelings pass into food and are passed on to those who consume it. Also the choice of the products with which one prepares to eat, or with which one eats is not a matter of little importance. We try to opt for natural ones, such as wood, or glass. However, wood has the problem of being inflammable and of absorbing tastes and odors, even those of detergent, therefore it is better to rinse it thoroughly under running water. However, each element has its peculiarities and must be treated with care.[29]

When we decide what to eat, let's listen and let us not be influenced by advertising. Let's try to understand what are the foods that we really want. That maybe that desire conceals a need of our body, which uses this means to communicate it to us. Vitamins, proteins, sugars. So, let's not take our culinary desires as mere whims.

Even the moment of consumption has its own rules. As we have seen when talking about breakfast, we try to think mainly about the meal and the diners, we turn off television, radio, cell phones and other electronic devices. Eventually, we can have the meal accompanied by good background music. We should be silent, and if we are eating with someone, our meal must have priority. We should eat calmly, catching all the flavors, all the smells and all the sounds of food. The Zen meal is synesthetic. Let's try to be elegant and to use well folded cloth napkins, crystal (at least) glasses and a gratifying tableware.

There are five meditations related to food and they are

1) The elements that make up food are the same as those that make up our body. When we eat something, we are eating a part of the universe.

1) The relationship between us and food is mutual and that's why when we eat we must be present

and aware

2) We need to understand what we really need and if while we're eating we are too busy talking to others or watching TV, this awareness can fail. Indeed, it will almost certainly fail.

3) Food must make us reflect on the fact that we are inextricably linked with the rest of humanity, because there have been people who cooked it and put their energy into it. Not to mention the rest of the supply chain.

4) We must be aware of the fact that what we eat will become part of our body, and for this we must honor it by using our body well, preferably doing good to others and living in harmony with them. Simply stated, if I were food, I would like to be eaten by a good person!

But we must also pay attention to the shopping phase, making it with awareness and without being conditioned by colored envelopes and offers. And when we cook, let's try to think of the most suitable recipe for our ingredients.

Even if we eat slowly, we will feel even more satisfied.

Three final considerations.

The first is that some of these councils are already becoming familiar to us For example, some cooking programs insist on combining multiple components and textures, though not like Zen. Another point on which the chefs insist is the plating and, as it happens, the presentation of the dishes is very important for Zen. However, those who practice Zen cannot appreciate certain excesses and certain freak scenes that are seen in these tv shows. Even the fact that there is a competition can't be seen with a good eye, because in a kitchen must reign harmony and not competition.

The second is that it is not very different from when in some families you decide to turn off the TV during lunch and/or dinner or when on Sunday we eat with the beautiful service. Except that for Zen we should try to do this every day.

For the third, I want to tell a personal episode. I had dinner at a kosher restaurant once. Being ignorant on the subject, I expected to find some kind of specialties, instead there were quite normal dishes, nothing shocking. Why this? Because cooking is above all a way of approaching food with an inner attitude, based on ideas or precepts. In the same way also Zen

We must understand that what we eat will transform it

into energy, but also into emotions. Borges wrote that every word contains the infinite. Likewise, every bite is full of life and its energy. We should be grateful because we couldn't survive without food, and we also need to reflect that we are luckier than many other people because we can eat every day and several times a day. We must be aware of it.

The Mindfulzen [30]

The Mindfulzen is a type of meditation created by Master Carlo Tetsugen Serra.[31]

It is thought to be difficult and complicated, this because the meditator puts the mind instead of the mental presence of the heart. Meditation in the MINDFULZEN is simple and easy, if you know how to breathe you can also meditate. Meditation is conscious observation of yourself and what you are experiencing. Meditation will not make you escape suffering, but will give you the tools to overcome it.

Meditation, especially Meditation in MINDFULZEN, concerns every moment of our life.

Every moment can be lived with awareness and through the kind observation of ourselves, every moment of life becomes unique and wonderful.

Therefore meditation is our whole life when we become aware of it.

Meditation is conscious observation of yourself and what you are experiencing. Meditation will not make you escape suffering, but will give you the tools to overcome it.

There are no particular moments

There are moments to eat, others to sleep, moments suitable for social relationships, and others for solitude, and others to affirm oneself; everything can have the best time to express itself, but every moment is the right one to know yourself, so don't wait for particular moments to be aware, but start from where you are here and now MINDFULZEN.

Meditating MINDFULZEN exercises the three fundamental qualities

Concentration

It helps to keep the mind firm in what you are doing, concentration enriches you with energy because it makes you live concentrated in the here and now. Being careful means becoming aware of what you are experiencing.

Exercising attention with meditation increases the ability to process present information in real time to become aware.

Awareness

The quality of our life depends on the degree of awareness with which we live it. The result of attention is awareness, if we are attentive and have an open heart and mind, we cannot help but be aware. Awareness is the bridge between us and reality.

Mindfulzen helps us to accept reality, helps us to choose what to do, in what to commit ourselves, to develop our values, benevolence and insight. It helps us to consider thoughts for what they are, thoughts, in fact, and not objective reality, and to keep them in mind without identifying ourselves with them. It helps us to take action to improve our lives and that of others, and of the environment around us.

There are eight Mindfulzen teachings: no judgment, patience, a beginner's mind, no expectations, acceptance, letting go and love

The four conscious truths:

- Life is wonderful, but it is characterized by suffering

- The origin of suffering is attachment to the self

- The elimination of attachment to the ego makes us stop suffering

- The awakening of the conscious mind ends the suffering.

The conscious mind has these characteristics:

Mental presence, investigation and search for wisdom, joy of being on the journey, favorable energy in mind and body, mind without stress of personal attainment, concentration, equal mind.

The eight attitudes of awareness or awareness free of preconceptions, thinking based on awareness, the word based on awareness, consciously acting in reality here and now, consciously living our lives with respect for others and in harmony with them, the awareness of having a mind conditioned by the ego, consciously engaging others, having the awareness of being interdependent with others, and being aware of our commitment to the reality of our journey.

We will thus arrive to behave ethically.

Awareness is also useful to consciousness. Thanks to it, our free and positive emotions will be released, and we will be more available towards others, and towards us. We will be free from fear and selfishness, from illusions and suffering.

Beyond meditation [32]

Whoever makes zen, who is a Buddhist or follows some principles, does not limit himself to meditating, but acts in order to make the world a better place.

Circulate your love

Among the moral actions of Zen that I like the most, there is the precept not to return the good to those who did it to us, but to do it to a third person. In this way, we will create a common good that will benefit many people. This is perfectly consistent with the Buddhist vision that sees us all bound and united by the fact of being made of the same essence, and by the fact of being transient. Therefore, let us try to do good. We are all interconnected.

Generosity and benevolence must not only concern human beings, but also other living beings. Even the plants. We are also interconnected with them.

Do you know the Zen phrase of one-handed sound? How do you interpret it? I do so: we need others, as one hand needs the other to make a sound come out.

We do good in a disinterested way, and sooner or later it will come back, says the Zen. We do not say that life is a spinning wheel, and that everything we do, whether good or bad, will be returned to us one day? And then, if not on this earth, at least we will have a reward in the Hereafter. But the Zen does not believe in the afterlife, and speaks of happiness and recognition already on this Earth. Indeed, only on this Earth, and wants happiness to be shared. For this reason there are ritual recurrences in which the sweets are offered to the Buddha and are shared with the neighbors.

To bring more happiness to the world we should learn to think big and do something useful for others. At the same time, we must not neglect small actions, both because the big actions are small actions (Scrooge McDuck docet with his Number One), and because a small action can do a lot. It can do a lot because it starts to improve the world, and because it can be taken as an example. Kant said: act as if your actions could become an example of universal b

In Milan, in Corso Buenos Aires, I saw a boy cleaning his street corner. He had a sign that said he wanted to keep that part of the world clean.

As I write this book, there is a lot of talk about a Swedish girl named Greta Thunberg, who with her perseverance moved the conscience of many of her peers.

Don't you find them both a little Zen? You too can do it.

Finally, don't you find that the use of suspended coffee is a small summary of all this?

Don't be afraid to make mistakes

An error is just a wrong approach to a question or problem. Each of them is nothing but a way to get to the right method. Indeed, for some questions we cannot even use the yes-no, true-false scheme because they are larger, and therefore need a more complex answer. In these cases, the Japanese respond with the word nu. In this case, one cannot even speak of a wrong answer.[33]

It tells of a school where students were invited to make more mistakes in order to be able to laugh about them in the future. In this way the fear of making a mistake would have been exorcised, and the mistakes would have been taken for what they are: attempts to reach the truth.[34]

Even in our culture we are quite lenient towards those who make mistakes. Just think of the proverbs "Error is only human" (which, however, is completed by the part that reads " but to persist in it, is diabolical!") and "Practice makes perfect". However, an ancient Greek motto reads: en pathei, mazon. In suffering, learning. The path to knowledge is not easy.

Dancing leaves

In Zen monasteries everything is regulated, and the monks know well in advance what they will have to do at a given time. They claim to be free only in this way, because they are no longer slaves of the moment and its contingency. I don't know, everyone adjusts as he believes.

I think a little bit about myself

When you are aware of reality and of yourself, deep love will be born within you for everything and for everyone, for all our beauty, as well as for all our imperfections. The compassionate state is born, a loving acceptance of everything. Love for yourself will turn into love towards every moment of life, and envelops everything you do, including people.[35]

Doing meditation, eating well, having fulfilling sex, having a garden, walking in Zen mode, are all ways to feel good. I want to add two.

We must gratify ourselves, and notice when we get success, when we do something positive. Some tend not to give weight to the good things they do, or to pass them over in silence. Instead, satisfaction frees dopamine, and dopamine stimulates the urge to do.

41

We must also forgive ourselves. Did we cheat, did we make a mistake? Be patience, we will fix that.

It seems to me that the meaning is quite clear: we must try to feel good, because that's what we strive to with others.

Also for our culture forgiveness (the forgiveness of sins) and the recognition of value are important, but we want them to come from third parties. Just blend in, says a proverb. Instead, Zen teaches us that we can be aware of our success and our value, without being snooty or old geezers.

Even those who absolve themselves, are not seen very well. Zen teaches us to forgive ourselves.

A little healthy selfishness helps altruism.

Our joy can shine in favor of others.

Seeing what hurts others can make us think about what is or is not necessary. After all, hasn't Buddhism started like this?

The teachings serve us just to understand the necessary things and the things that can also be done without.

Paradoxically, Zen tells us that if we conquer the firmness of the mind we can afford not to completely detach ourselves from earthly things.

Another paradox: the desire not to have attachments to

earthly pleasures risks becoming an attachment in itself. Zen does not want us to become moralists or ascetics.

Take advantage of what we don't like about us

Let's go over this one more time: the Zen states that we must accept the things that we don't like. Here, however, we are taking a shot: we must try to make it a strong point. Like the nun who painted with her mouth.

Another nun (the first American Buddhist nun) wrote that we must feed our demons to draw strength from them.[36]

Garrincha, a Brazilian player, had one leg shorter than the other and the lameness made it easier to dribble through opponents. Too bad that not everyone knows how to dribble, or play in the Brazilian national team.

Maybe we get a little closer to this Zen idea with resilience. Sometimes there is also awareness.

Examples of closeness between the two cultures

Are Western and Zen culture really that far? The word creates the world, and throughout the book I will give you examples that can show you that many of the things we do, or that are part of our Western culture, already have something of Zen in them and could make our journey easier. But we lack the awareness of it, and someone to help us do it. Only then can we say: "I am doing something applying the principles of Zen".

There is a writer who can represent a trait-d-union between the West and Japan, and she is the Belgian Amelie Nothomb. The daughter of a diplomat, she was born and raised in Japan, even though she left her native country when she was a child and followed her father in China and other Far Eastern countries. The latter makes some mention in a book called "Biography of Hunger" and elsewhere, but Japan, one of its rockstar literary production (really prolific) and Nothomb makes us know many aspects, even grotesque and paradoxical. In fact, I discovered aspects of Japan that I didn't really know by reading Nothomb's books. I would like to focus on one step. In "Metaphysics of the tubes", she, an unmanageable child, is calmed by a piece of Belgian white chocolate.[37]

Have you seen Kill Bill, Quentin Tarantino's eastern western? Do you remember the scene in which the Bride (Uma Thurman, for instance), wakes up after a very long coma? What moves first thing? The feet. This has a very Zen meaning, and we must not exclude that the reference is wanted, given the director's interest in that culture.

Drieu La Rochelle[38] he was a French writer who went down in history because he was a Nazi, a Stalinist, a collaborator and a suicide seeker. He wanted to annihilate his own self to merge with the universal whole. Although not very edifying, it is another example of closeness between the West and the East. Isn't one of the principles of Buddhism Nirvana, that is, the place where all subjectivity is lost?

Anyone who has studied a bit of philosophy knows that much importance is given to the senses as data collectors that the mind then reworks, and also knows that our mind shapes the shape of the world. Man is the measure of all things, is a principle of Renaissance philosophy, and finds its analogue in one of Zen.

He also knows in the early days that he sought the first principle, the element of which all beings are constituted. Thales hypothesized that it was water.

Excluding for reasons diametrically opposed Thales and the Nothomb, we do not know if the cases we have seen above derive from a knowledge of oriental culture, or anyway of an influence, or if they are simply the result of a coincidence (another principle dear to Zen) and, ultimately, we don't even care. What interested us was the fact that we are not so far away, and we will return in the course of the book. We understand that some things we do are already zen, only that we need to work on it.

Zen, Network and the world

We mentioned before the vegan cook imitated by Maurizio Crozza. Now let's talk about another character from the Genoese comedian, Napalm 51. Who is Napalm 51? Napalm 51 represents the haters. The haters, the word itself says it, but surely you will already know it, they are people who vent their anger on the Internet, especially on social networks. We leave out the question of fake news because it goes beyond this context, even if the two concepts are often linked, and let's focus on anger. If Napalm 51 began to listen to their own feelings, even the negative ones, they would be able to understand and accept them, finding a more peaceful way of expressing and controlling them. Because we all have moments of anger, and anger must not be repressed, but we must only not let it turn into rage.

The main point is that for Zen every man is

46

enlightened, only that all those obstacles that prevent the light from radiating must be eliminated. Zen and practices help us do it. In this way, the hater character created by Crozza would stop insulting, and even click and share compulsively. The abuse of the Internet that many do is a form of greed 2.0. Also for this reason the Zen advises to switch off the mobile devices from time to time, at least during meals. It absolutely does not ask to live without, because it has fallen into the world and is indeed a way to live better within it. Why, let it be known, "The Buddha, the Divine, dwells in the circuit of a computer or in the gears of the change of a motorcycle with the same ease as atop a mountain or in the petals of a flower".[39]

Zen does not even want us to renounce pleasure and gratification, or that we punish ourselves in penance. It simply tells us that we must seek the source of happiness within us, so that it is more stable and more lasting. Events outside of us can change, indeed they will almost certainly change and some will be painful. If we entrust our happiness exclusively to the outside world, when things go wrong, how will we do it? On the contrary, the happiness that comes from within will not be subject to so many changes. Let's take it as a useful tip. But do you advise us to be insensitive to the pain of others or not to feel them? Absolutely not. Pain exists, it must be accepted and Zen helps us do it.

Of course, superficial things can give us pleasure, and

pleasure should not be rejected, but we will find true happiness by coming into harmony with our deepest part.

Jung spoke of me and The Self, and for him dreams are the bridge between the two components of our personality, while for Zen it is meditation.

Answer to the objections of the previous chapter

Someone will dispute: but if we already have these habits, why bring up Zen? I refer above all to that of counting up to ten. Because there is a difference, which is that we understand that Zen has negative feelings, and we accept them. We say that it is as if there were a sort of splitting thanks to which we perceive our negative part (or obscure, as some claim). We are aware of this. In general, some uses that we have in the West or that we are adopting in the West are bricks that help us build our Zen home, but we must also put other types of bricks and, what matters most, the house will be special. In short, it is not enough to put chopsticks to be a Japanese restaurant. We must also pay attention to the elements that we have and which they lack, and also to understand that in some cases it is a structural non-presence. I refer to the almost total absence of speculation, as we have already seen. A bit like a fat-free kitchen. Amelie

Nohthomb said that Japanese monuments are built and designed to be admired in the dark.[40]. One more case in which the absence of something, in this case the light of the sun, becomes structural.

The second objection is that there are ways to channel anger, such as sport and artistic sublimation. Well, those who already succeed in these ways, probably don't need Zen. The point is that Zen is not only useful for managing anger and aggression.

A bit of pop

Zen and sex

Zen is not bigot. It does not condemn homosexuality and neither does sex only for pleasure. He recognizes it as an integral part of life, and invites only to do it with awareness and respect for other people. He does not condemn even those who resort to prostitution, or those who resort to masturbation. Above all with regard to the latter, he knows that it is a natural thing and asks only that it be done in a balanced way, avoiding disorders, excesses and upsets. What is the limit? Everyone must understand their own.

Moreover, it could not be otherwise: not having a metaphysical basis and, above all, not having a transcendent idea, it certainly cannot have a rigid moral doctrine in certain fields of self related to subjectivity and individual choices such as food and sexuality. Let's say that Zen gives us advice on how to live better, not precepts.

Zen, and in general all Buddhism, in the sexual sphere leaves to the laity freedom. He only asks that one not deal with people who are engaged or married, with mental patients and with prisoners or ex-prisoners. He also asks, and that is what matters most, that people and their happiness are placed at the center of everything, therefore also of the sexual sphere. I do not agree with the ban on having sex with former prisoners, given that once a sentence has been served a person regains the right to a normal life, without talking about the consequences. As you can see, I have a detached approach to this practice and this religion.

This time I will not write conclusions to the chapter by making parallels between Western and Zen behavior, but I add a note of color: Jennifer Aniston [41] is a fan of Zen sex.

I want to add a sort of quote instead. Have you seen the movie Sex and Zen? I did, and found it quite grotesque, but in retrospect it was simply ironic. Irony as a detachment, which is one of the cornerstones of Buddhism. We also find a desire to overcome and learn, but learn in a practical way, for concrete things, in full Zen style.[42]

A Buddhist sutra states: do not waste love and sex, and literature on Zen and sex is not lacking.

Another Buddhist thought holds that passions are a road to enlightenment.

Osho[43] ha wrote a book entitled "Secrets and mysteries of eros"[44]. It seems to me that space is given to this human component, and without condemnations or morbidity. What do you think about it?

The Zen gardens

In an episode of the cartoon, the Simpsons set up a Zen garden. This is my first memory of these Japanese wonders, in which one goes to meditate, and which do not have an aesthetic function. The elements and their arrangement constitute a fundamental part of it. Great importance is given to water, to which zen itself attaches great importance.

The Japanese name with which the Zen gardens are indicated is Karesansui, which means *"stone gardens"*. Its origins date back to Japanese Shintoism. Buddhist monks have taken over Japanese gardens to have a space within the monasteries where they can meditate and pray better. But it is possible can create this corner of peace in which to reflect even in non-religious places..[45] From a religious point of view, the Japanese garden is **naturocentric** (unlike the Western one, which is defined as anthropocentric), **asymmetrical** and **apparently random**; expresses the harmony of man with nature. Each element corresponds to something. The sand symbolizes water and the stones symbolize the islands. We have to make drawings on the sand that imitate the waves. The stones must always be odd, and above all never four, because the Japanese associate it with death. [46] It is preferable that a Zen garden is small and fenced. Care must be taken constantly, but doing it is not difficult because they are "dry gardens", which need little water.[47]

In this way we can enter the discourse of Zen minimalist architecture, and think that even our architecture, and above all our design are becoming very minimalist [48]. Let's also consider local buildings like the Bosco Verticale in Milan.

Can't you see a Zen influence here too?

The carps

Those of you who have ever played Pokémon Go, played with cards, or have seen the cartoon, will surely remember Magikarp. What is it? It is a very weak fish that evolves into Gyarados, a dragon that is also one of the most fearsome Pokémon. according to legend there is a waterfall and the carps that go beyond it become dragons. In fact, the creators were inspired by this legend. What does it mean? It means that everyone has the chance to make a qualitative leap, and to become an enlightened person. Indeed, to return to it.

This does not seem sacrilegious: the Japanese are used to using cartoons to spread the culture, and to make children approach you too. Think for example of Lady Oscar and Pollon.

Even the Buddhist deities choose unusual and unexpected ways to reach their goal. Bodhisattva Kuan Yin, who represents the feminine energy of compassion took the form of a seductive fisherwoman and promised to marry those who had learned some sutras. After a while he died, and he made his husband promise to remember her by spreading the teaching of the Buddha.[49]

Some interesting facts [50]

When they enter the convent the monks make an offer for their own funeral.

The Buddhist temple is called sangha.

In Japanese, the prolonged retreats in which one meditates are called sesshin, which translates as a "union of minds", while in Korean the expression is "yong meng Jong non", meaning "when you're sitting, jump like a tiger". The newly appointed monk is called a shukke, a homeless monk.

The monks vow to follow the eight teachings of the Buddha (also called The Eightfold Path). Eight meditations that must be learned with the heart, and put into practice. They are right view, right resolve, right speech, right livelihood, right effort, right mindfulness, and right samadhi ('meditative absorption or union').

The silence is very important thanks to which we will enter into harmony with the deepest part of us, and will awaken compassion, empathy, tenderness and love. They promote happiness.

Tenzo is the monk who takes care of the kitchen. He wakes up before the others to eat, and goes to bed last after fixing everything. Our culture considers those who serve others to be of lower rank, whereas in the Zen monasteries the tenzo is second only to the prior of the convent in hierarchy.

More questions

Are there Zen monasteries in Italy?

Yes, there are eight. One in Milan, one in Berceto (Pr), one in Brescia, one in Cantù (Co), one in Cecina (Li), one in Padua, one in Naples and one in Avellino. Some are open to the laity, who can go and spend a few days to experience the zen with the monks.

What do we owe to Zen?

The haiku poetic form, the tea ceremony, the art of arranging flowers (ikebana), the art of calligraphy (shodō), painting (zen-ga), Japanese theater (Nō), culinary art (zen-ryōri, shojin ryōri, fucharyōri), martial arts such as aikido, judo and karate, the art of the sword (kendō) and archery (kyūdō)[51]. But also in the kitchen field, with zen-ryori, shojin-ryori and fucha-ryori. If you think about it, the dishes we eat at the Japanese restaurant are made with the ingredients we've seen to be the basis of Zen food, and we're not just referring to food.[52]

Where is the oldest Zen temple in the world?

The oldest Zen temple in the world is Tofuku-ji and is located in Kyoto and dates back to the 12th century.

When did Zen spread in the West?

It is difficult to say, but certainly an important period is the end of the 19th century. It is certain that the first official conversion was that wife of Alexander Russel in 1906. A very important role was given by Daisets Teitaro Suzuki (1869-1955), with her books, of which we remember the Essays in Zen Buddhism.[53]

The Zenroma website reports instead:

Spread over the centuries from India to China to Japan, and then throughout Asia, it arrived in Europe, France, through Master Taisen Deshimaru in 1967 and is now practiced and known throughout the world.[54]

Do Zen nuns exist?

Yes of course.

Experiences, stories and anecdotes

Welcome to the most creative part of the book, where you will find some personal inspiration.

Zen, football and archery

Andrea played football, and dreamed of making a memorable goal, but no matter how hard he tried, though he resigned himself to crossing the posts, despite having a correct body posture, and trying to calibrate the shot well. He didn't have square feet, yet he couldn't. Even one would have been enough, even if people said it was the "best Sunday goal", which was just luck.

He changed many coaches, but with all he had the same result. He was good, but he was thinking of quitting.

Then one day he came across a Japanese. Yes it was a Zen football master, who told him "You have to understand that you don't have to aim for the seven, and you don't have to think about how you put the body or what part of the foot you hit the ball. You just have to learn to breathe well, that's the key to everything. "

Andrea tried it out in a game: he breathed the way the Japanese master had taught him, kicked the ball without thinking too much, and a masterpiece came out of it.

It was not only thanks to the technique that he succeeded, but above all to the fact of not having thought of the gesture, of having done it by creating the void, and merging consciousness and unconscious. He had outgrown the technique, and the technique had become an inapprehensive art, gushed from the unconscious.[55]

Andrea made that great goal by performing a Zen action. What do you mean? In the sense that he did it in a natural way without thinking too much on how to do that.

The Japanese are not very good at playing football, on the other hand they are good at shooting with a bow, and they know that you become skilled archers, only when the mind stops focusing on the details of what it is doing. Only in this way, the technique learned will come out.

And it can come out because it has become introjected, it has become ours, indeed, it has become a part of us.

The Japanese are not very good at playing soccer

(although they have improved a lot lately), but years ago they created a cartoon in "Japan wins the world championship"[56]. Yes it is Holly and Benji, as many of you have guessed. Well, the champion Holly often said this sentence: "The ball is your friend". Because with friends we can be natural and do things without thinking about it, naturally. And those with friends are moments when we are free, and we offer the best part of us. But the ball does not become everyone's friend and above all it does not become a friend immediately, except in very rare cases. We need to become familiar with it. In this respect it is not very dissimilar from the Japanese bow, which is not immediately given immediately, but requires so much exercise. They are similar also for another fact: just as a good shooter with an average value bow shoots an arrow better than a mediocre shooter with a higher bow, in the same way a good footballer will do more dribbles with a normal ball, than a poor one with a latest-generation ball. Above all, the two good ones will almost certainly do it thinking less than the less gifted ones.[57]

What interests us is the naturalness that is achieved only when we are completely detached from ourselves, and that it is one with the perfection of technical ability. It is when things come to us very well, not "though we don't think" but "because we don't think about it".

In one passage of the book 'Zen and archery', the master strikes in a room lit only by a very dim light, first the target, and then with a second arrow, the first arrow. It hits them from a very respectable distance. It is not only a question of technique, but also of introjected technique, which allows you to pull as you pull. In another part of the book, the master gets angry with the protagonist, because he uses a shortcut based only on technique, concentrating excessively on what he is doing.

Zen focuses on a gesture: breathing. Breathing that moves our inner life. We a little less.[58]

Painters and zen

I once spoke with a Milanese artist. He marveled at the many meanings I managed to find in his works. He told me that the images went directly from the unconscious to his hand. Of course I don't know how to paint, so I look for hidden meanings in artistic works. In addition he, like almost all artists, was concrete, not speculative, lived his own art and in this sense was more zen than the best. Best: it was potentially, in the philosophical meaning of power, more zen than me.

Have you ever talked to an artist, especially a painter? It can be very disappointing, especially if one had the illusion of learning some hidden meaning of the picture, in particular details, some elements or chromatic choices. Often they are of a disarming simplicity, and all this can be twice Zen. First of all, because it teaches us the value of self-practice. The painter paints the picture because he likes that image or idea, or because he was commissioned. It has an overview of the picture, then the details come later, you will think about it. Although the most delicious aspects of the works are often linked to the details. From Caravaggio who used prostitutes as models for sacred figures, to Luini who gave a woman who was about to be delivered the face of an ex-lover, from the Judas of Leonardo who would have the appearance of the prior, to the many anonymous girls who , as Sebastiano Vassalli informs us, just as anonymous madonnas did pose to paint precisely the Madonna. End of the digression, let's get back to us and our Zen. Disarming artists can be on the zen path for another reason. Because they don't think, they don't think speculatively and rationally, but they think, like the rain that falls. According to a way of saying, those who can't do, teach. Here, painters know how to do, so they don't teach. And whoever does not even know how to teach is a critic and finds senses that have even escaped the author himself. He had the key element, which is naturalness. Because he had introjected his art.

A few years ago I followed a tai-chi lesson. While I practiced some positions, I reflected on the fact that they are not so different from movements that we can do in our gym or at home doing some physical activity. The same happened to me with the position of the warrior during stretching. But there were more elements. The first is poetry, which we miss a little. There is a difference between doing a lunge and making the position of a warrior. The second. it is concentration on what you are doing. Not that we miss you, but I perceived it differently there. We focus on repetitions, loads, posture, recovery time. In tai-chi, I perceived attention to the gesture in its entirety, and it was so beautiful that you hardly noticed that you were doing things you can do even in the gym. Have you ever seen children play empty sack full bag? They enjoy carefree, but they are doing squats.

Who is an expert on Zen, would say that we are faced with examples of Satori, in which the differences between subject and object, and between conscience and unconscious cancel each other out. It is not an immediate thing. Therefore, here is a more appropriate explanation to us;

Zen culture is closely linked to gesture, to repetition as perfection, to the moment when thought is nullified, and only action counts. It is a philosophy that is applied in many disciplines related to Japanese culture, in which the hand that draws a mark with the brush can be the same as holding a kendo sword. **There is no hesitation within a pure Zen gesture,**

because that gesture has become so much a part of you, that your body executes it without the mind being involved. **It is the muscle memory of the athlete who does not think, but acts.** Yoda's motto of Star Wars, which not by chance incorporates within itself the appearance, ways and many of the philosophies of a Zen master, was **"Do or Do not, there is no Try"**.[59]

In Summary

Zen Buddhism (or better, Dharma, as it is known in the East) is a Japanese school that came to Japan thanks to the expansion of the Mahayana doctrine (great vehicle), or an anti-substantialistic and anti metaphysical philosophy (birth and death are Nirvana, illusions are illumination) which denies dualism. Zen is a monastic tradition based on the lineage (transmission of dharma from master to disciple), martial and very Japanese, made of rituals sometimes a bit complicated, anti-intellectual, and with a taste for paradox (koans). Essential and practical discipline, it has produced the aesthetics that we recognize as peculiar to Japan (the gardens, the minimal and very illuminated spaces).

The fundamental formal practice is zazen, or sitting meditation. Other practices are walking meditation, and particular rituals that mark the fundamental stages of the journey, or discipline (dharma or dhamma in pali means discipline, rule, law and many other things). Attention to food, from preparation to presentation, conviviality, and no room for intellectual speculation.

The lineage is what is transmitted from master to disciple, and this happens not through words but through observation.

The Buddhist Zen doctrine is founded like the same Chán Buddhism from which it strictly derives, on the refusal to recognize authority to the Buddhist scriptures (_sutra_[60]).

This does not mean that Zen rejects the Buddhist scriptures. Indeed, some of them, such as the _Heart Sutra_, the _Vimalakīrti Nirdeśa Sūtra_ or the same _Laṅkāvatārasūtra_.

Zen avoids intellectual speculation, and is also distinguished from other Mahāyāna Buddhist schools for having centralized the meditative practice (_zazen_) in its _shikantaza_ forms (meditation on breath, mind and emptiness, performed by sitting) or accompanied by study of the _kōan_.

Appendix

Examples of Koan

A monk asked Chao-chou: "I entered this monastery right now. I ask the patriarch to explain the doctrine to me ».
Chao-chou replied, "Have you already eaten your boiled rice?"
The monk said, "I've already eaten it."
Chao-chou said, "Then go and wash the bowl."
The monk was enlightened.

To see clearly our image, we just need to clean the mirror

**

If you can't do anything, what can you do?

***

The master asked, "Who is hindering you?" The student: "Nobody hinders me". The master replied: "So, what need is there to seek liberation?"

***

A monk asked Chao-Chou: "If a poor man comes, what should he be given?" "He lacks nothing," replied the master.

***

If we move the boulders, the river will also change its course.

***

You can bring the thirsty ox to the river, but if he does not drink, he will die.

***

The fundamental illusion of humanity is to assume that I am here, and you are there.

***

We meditate on what we really want. Ave

Appendix 2

"The purpose of the Zen" (D. T. Suzuki)

Let's read for the last time some excerpts from the first volume of Essays on Zen Buddhism by D.T. Suzuki:

"The state in which every remnant of conceptual consciousness has vanished is called a state of poverty by Christian mystics. The definition of Tauler is: "Absolute poverty is in you, when you do not know how to remember if someone owes you something, or if you owe something to someone: just as everything will be forgotten by you, in the final journey of death".

[...] Wu-men (Mumon) sings:

Ten thousand flowers in spring, the moon in autumn,
a cool breeze in summer, snow in winter.
If your mind isn't clouded by unnecessary things,
this is the best season of your life.

Here other verses, by Shou-an (Shuan):

At Nantai I sit quietly with an incense burning,

One day of rapture, all things are forgotten,
Not that mind is stopped and thoughts are put away,
But that there is really nothing to disturb my serenity.

[...]The disciple of Zen [...] can be fully active [...] - and yet his spirit is filled with a happiness and a transcendent calm. [...] All the desires have fallen from his heart, no vain thought obstructs the flow of vital activity, and so he is empty and "poor". In his poverty he knows how to enjoy "spring flowers" and "autumnal moon". Until worldly riches were accumulated in his heart, there was no place for this transfigured joy. [...]

The purpose of Zen is to achieve what is technically called the "non-acquisition" state. All knowledge is acquisition and accumulation, while Zen aims to free us from all possession. The spirit must make us poor and humble, completely free of inner impurities. Instead, knowledge is rich and arrogant. [...]Zen certainly adheres to what Lao-tze says (*Tao-te-ching*, XLVIII): « Those who seek knowledge are enriched day by day. The one who seeks the Tao becomes poor from day to day. It becomes increasingly poor as long as it reaches non-action (*wu-wei*). With non-acting, there is nothing he cannot reach». In its perfection, this kind of loss is the "non-acquisition", identical to poverty. In poverty, one can see a synonym of "emptiness", of *sunyata*. When the spirit has purged itself of all the waste accumulated since time immemorial, the clothes fall, the trappings fall, only a naked essence remains. Now empty, free, authentic, the spirit assumes its innate dignity. And in this there is also joy, but not the joy that can give rise to its opposite, to sadness, but an absolute joy [...].

In Christianity, we think too much about God, although it is said that in him we live, we move and we have our being. Zen also wants the last trace of a dualistic consciousness of God to be erased. For this reason, it urges its followers not to stop even where the Buddha is and to pass quickly where there is no longer any Buddha " (dal cap. VII, par. XI).

(http://www.lameditazionecomevia.it/suzuki14.htm)

Appendix 3

I will end with a story taken from 101 Zen Stories (https://www.visioneolistica.it/contadino-saggio-storie-zen/).

Meanwhile, read it, then I'll explain.
Here is the story of the wise peasant.

Once upon a time in a Chinese village there was an old farmer who lived with his son and a horse, which was their only source of income.

One day, the horse escaped leaving the man without the possibility of working the land.

His neighbors came to him to show them their solidarity and said they felt sorry for the incident.

He thanked them for the visit, but asked them: "How do you know if what happened to me is good or bad for me? Who knows!"

The neighbors, perplexed by the old farmer's attitude, went away.

A week later the horse returned to the stable, accompanied by a large herd of horses. When the news reached the villagers, they returned to the farmer's house, congratulating him on his good fortune.

"Before you had only one horse, and now you have many. It is a great wealth. What luck! "They said.

"Thanks for the visit and for your solidarity," he replied, but how do you know that this is good or bad for me? "

The neighbors were once again baffled by the old farmer's response, and left.

Some time later, the farmer's son, in an attempt to tame one of the new horses, fell off and broke his leg.

The attentive neighbors returned to visit the farmer, proving to be very sorry for the misfortune.

The man thanked for the visit and affection of all, and again asked: "How can you know if the incident is a disgrace? Let's wait and see what happens over time. "

Once again, the old farmer's phrase left everyone stunned, and without words, they left in disbelief.

A few months passed, and Japan declared war on China. The government sent its emissaries throughout the country in search of healthy young men to send to the front in battle. They arrived at the village and recruited all the young men, except the farmer's son who had a broken leg.

None of the boys came back alive. The farmer's son instead recovered, and the horses were sold with a good income.

The wise farmer went to visit his neighbors to console and help them, as they had shown solidarity with him in every situation.

Whenever some of them complained, the wise farmer said, "How do you know if this is bad?" If someone rejoiced too much, he asked him: "How do you know if this is good?"

It was at that moment that the men of the village understood the teaching of the wise farmer who urged them not to get excited and **not let themselves be overwhelmed by events, always accepting what is**, aware of the fact that, <u>beyond good and evil</u>, **everything it may be different from what it looks like**.

First of all, I decided to add this story because I read it in the book "Siamo tutti latinisti" by Cesare Marchi. I didn't know it was a Zen story, but the mixture of West and East was one of the main themes of this book. Secondly, because as a writer I always have to deal with texts. Finally, because even writing (not in the sense of calligraphy) can be zen.

Our mind can and must be full of ideas, doubts and uncertainties, before and after writing. But when you start writing, all of this disappears and becomes immediate action. For us, the artist, the genius, is what creates a unique piece, the concept of absolute originality compared to previous works and the same rules of gender, is a contemporary concept, born with romanticism. Classical art was largely serial, and the historical avant-gardes have challenged in different ways the romantic idea of creation as an absolute debut.

Repetition is essential for Zen philosophy, as it is the only way to reach perfection. The way of Zen is a journey made of patience, perseverance and self-criticism. A journey that may seem far from a varied and creative activity such as writing, but it is not necessarily the case. What in Zen remains unchanged is the gesture and the execution. Everything else changes, and we can adapt to change, only if we are totally in control of ourselves.

Before and after writing, our mind can and must be full of ideas, doubts, uncertainties, these are the main ingredients that allow our creativity. However, when we place our hands on the keyboard or pick up a pen, all of this shall disappear to become an often unconscious flow. That is the secret and beautiful alchemy that drives people to tell you "where do you get your ideas?"

It is a thought that is linked in part to what we have already seen regarding creativity. Writing must be an almost monastic exercise, a ritual made up of repetitions in which we slowly prepare our brains to step aside to make room for that part of us that allows us to bring out the concept we want to express without having to think about it. He is there, we just have to reach him and express it through writing.

There will be enough time to correct that sentence we don't like or to delete that concept, but the heart of what we write is there, and we have already found it. This is fundamental, especially in these times when the work of writing on the internet often requires very short execution times, articles that must be precise, concise and well written right away. It also binds to the idea of a workout that lasts for years, but that bears fruit just when it's needed. A perfect and totally natural execution that hides years and years of mistakes and preparation.

Because luck exists, but it cannot be the only port to which a writer must refer. Luck is often just a synonym of preparation. For that moment when the train has passed, and you had your suitcase ready after training for years and years to prepare it perfectly.[61]

[1] A Zen master who died in 788- Cf.. Daisetz T. Suzuki, "Introduzione" to Eugen Herrigel, "Lo Zen e il tiro con l'arco", Adelphi, Milano, 1975, p.12.

[2] Fabrizio De Andrè, "Verranno a chiederti del nostro amore" (Fabrizio De Andrè-Nicola Piovani-Giuseppe Bentivoglio).

[3] American writer of German and Swedish origins born in 1928.

[4]Robert M. Pirsig, "Lo Zen e l'arte della manutenzione della motocicletta", Adelphi, Milano, 1981, p.395.

[5] http://www.treccani.it/enciclopedia/zen/

[6] http://www.zenroma.it/zen/

[7] Bodhidharma, whose life and work are located between the 5th and the 6th century AD, is one of the most indecipherable characters. The legends about him are as numerous as the verifiable historical sources are scarce. Among the few reliable data is its origin: he came from a noble family of South India. Another certain fact is his lineage, that of the XXVIII Patriarch of Buddhism, therefore a direct descendant of Siddharta Gautama (http://www.casamushin.it/bodhidharma.html)

[8] http://www.monasterozen.it/monastero-zen-il-cerchio/cosa-e-lo-zen/

[9] https://www.laciviltacattolica.it/articolo/esercizio-zen-e-meditazione-cristiana/

[10] By slightly modifying the phrase of the Viscount Cobram, the total director of Fantozzi, a fanatic of cycling, we can say that Zen is a healthy activity for everyone and from which everyone can benefit. If instead you prefer a more courtly quote, here's what Suzuki writes (see note 1) "The characteristic diversity between Zen and all other religious, philosophical or mystical doctrines, is the fact that Zen never leaves our daily life, and that, despite all the range of its practical applications of its concreteness, it has something in itself that places it outside the contamination and tumult of the theater of the world.

[11] A koan states: "Before the awakening I cut wood and carried water;
after waking up I cut wood and carried water. "We'll see what the koans are next.
[12]

http://www.gianfrancobertagni.it/materiali/zen/buddismozen.htm
[13] Nansen Osho, "Lezioni del Buddha per raggungere la serenità in 3 mesi. 90 esercizi per rendere meravigliosa la vita di tutti i giorni". Antonio Vallardi Editore, Milano, 2015, p.215.
[14] https://www.ipermind.com/filosofia-zen/
[15] I don't specify because in reality the phrase has been attributed to several people.
[16] Nan-in, a Japanese master of the Meiji era (1868-1912), received a visit from a university professor who had come to him to question him about Zen.
Nan-in served tea. He filled his guest's cup, and then continued to pour.
The professor watched as the tea spilled over, then he could no longer contain himself. «It is full. It no longer has anything to do with it! "
"Like this cup," said Nan-in, "you are filled with your opinions and conjectures. How can I explain Zen to you if you don't empty your cup first?
".(https://buddhismoitalia.forumcommunity.net/?t=55499193)
[17] In the book by Amélie Nothomb "Neither of Eve nor of Adam" there is a passage in which we talk about the fact that even in schools pupils are not used to asking questions. Instead she, who is European, asks them and it creates discomfort and embarrassment.
[18] The importance of this simple and natural gesture crosses cultures. Consider the Greek "pneuma", which indicates the breath and the vital breath, or the fact that God breathes into Adam, and he comes to life.
[19] Nansen Osho, op. cit. , pp. 212-3.

[20] Zazen means sitting meditation. To practice zazen you don't need any particular physical requirements, zazen is within everyone's reach and basically its essence lies in the fact of being "simply sitting" in a posture that facilitates concentration from which greater self-awareness is derived. During the meditation one remains seated and in silence, concentrating on breathing, on the natural coming and going of the breath, only observing it. In the same way one observes the rising and passing of thoughts, and without attachment one lets them go. Even if for many meditation is something strange, transcendent, incomprehensible, in reality it belongs to each of us, from the beginning and it is only a different way of making our body-spirit work. Beyond its spiritual and philosophical connotations, Zen is by now learned and used as a benevolent support to manage anxiety, stress and all those coercion mechanisms that make life today so difficult. Today, more than ever, techniques like Mindfulness, body relaxation, Yoga and other forms of support and development of awareness are increasingly used to free man from the burden of everyday life.

[21] https://www.meditazionezen.it/cose-la-meditazione-zen-2/

[22] A koan is literally, the transcription of a "public case" that happened in the past; or, as a Zen master said, "the place where truth is found". Generally speaking, koans are taken from authentic dialogues between Zen masters and students, or between advanced practitioners, or from sutras or ancient sayings. Most of the time, koans are paradoxical in nature, and cannot be understood by the intellect. Thus, a koan can only be understood thanks to the direct experience of the authentic mind from which it was born. The sayings and dialogues that turned into koans are collected in various texts, such as the Mumonkan. Some scholars assert that in the early days many people chose the practice of koan to learn to cope with the sufferings of their lives. The koan offers the opportunity for a solid practice, not only while sitting in zazen, but also in the midst of the turmoil of life. It provides the concrete means to break the bond of suffering in

times of conflict and uncertainty.
(http://www.fiorediloto.org/koan.htm)

[23] Wikipedia simply translates it into just sitting

[24] The word Zazen Shikantaza: "simply sitting" means that we sit in zazen with simplicity, without goals and expectations. The secret and the difficulty lie precisely in this word: simply. When we sit in zazen, in fact, we abandon knowledge and knowledge and enter naked into the practice of being.
Shikantaza, that is to witness the reality of one's being. In Zen it is said, in fact, "Enter in Zazen, and you do not go out any more": it means that when you sit in meditation, you do it with your baggage of illusions and conditionings, thoughts and expectations, then your illusion of being a small separate me vanishes, and here is no one sitting in Zazen anymore, you are no longer as you thought before, but a universal being as you are now.

[25] https://martaalbe.com/2017/03/29/meditazione-sassolini/

[26] The meditation and breathing practices described in this book, including the shikantaza and the koan described above, are taken by Master Tetsugen Serra, "Zen 3.0, Cairo Editore, Milano, 2015, passim. Unless otherwise indicated.

[27] Cf. Nansen Osho, op. cit.

[28] Germidi Soia.

[29] For materials, cf Simone Martinelli, Zenstation, Piacere in tutti i sensi, Lit Srl-Ultra Edition, Roma, 2015, pp.57-68.

[30] http://mindfulzen.it/la-meditazione-mindfulzen/

[31] Milano, 1953-vivente. Cf. op. cit. Being the creator of the Mindfulzen, the part inherent to this discipline is taken from the parts of his book in which he speaks about it.

[32] Cf. Nansen Osho, op. cit. The next five chapters have this book as a main reference.

[33] Zen is said in the book, and the art of motorcycle maintenance.

[34] Osho reports it in the cited book.

[35] http://mindfulzen.it/la-meditazione-mindfulzen/

[36] Tsultrim Allione, "Nutri i tuoi demoni. Risolvere i conflitti interiori con la saggezza del Buddha". Oscar Mondadori, Milano, 2009.

[37] I wanted to understand chocolate as a gift from the world to the child to repair the fracture that had been created, to tell her that she wanted to welcome it. A sort of primordial element.

[38] Cf. Drieu La Rochelle, Racconto Segreto-Diario 1944-45 SE Editore, 2005.

[39] Robert M. Pircing, op. cit.

[40] In "Happy nostalgia".

[41] http://www.oggi.it/people/vip-e-star/2011/08/10/jennifer-aniston-il-sesso-zen-e-un-traguardo-importante/

[42] https://it.wikipedia.org/wiki/Sex_and_Zen_-_Il_tappeto_da_preghiera_di_carne

[43] Not the one mentioned above, but the best-known Osho, also famous for the fake phrases that run on the Net. This Osho was born in 1931 and died in 1980 and was Indian, the former is Japanese and is alive. Moreover, as regards the latter, on the second "o" there is a sign, similar to that of long vowels, which I couldn't sign.

[44] Universale Economica Feltrinelli, Milano, 2015. Pagg. 80.

[45] But it is also true that for Zen every place can be a place to meditate, and every situation can be a starting point for reflection on life and the true importance of material goods.

[46]

https://luomodimezzanotte.wordpress.com/2015/03/14/tetrafobia-la-paura-del-numero-4/

[47] Cf. https://www.ilgiardinodeilibri.it/speciali/il-giardino-zen-giardinaggio-religione-filosofia.php

[48] Everything can be inspired by Zen, as we can understand from this article.

In Zen philosophy the house obviously occupies a place of

prestige, because it is the place where you spend more time and where you can recharge the energy that modern times take us away. Transforming your apartment into a corner of tranquility thanks to Zen principles will lead you to think more clearly and to better face everyday challenges.

Furnishing the house according to the Zen philosophy means creating a simple and orderly environment with few furnishing accessories, with essential lines. Always choose furniture and organic products - wood must be the king of the house - The lines to choose are square, clean and essential and with few decorations.

https://donnad.prod.h-art.it/a-casa/casa-e-arredo/interni/filosofia-giapponese-zen-cos-e-e-quali-sono-i-principi.

[49] Master Tetsugen Serra, op. cit. pp. 205-206.

[50] Cf. Master Tetsugen, op. cit.

[51] Someone will be surprised by the zen-martial arts approach, but here is a step that explains their relationship well: Zen in Martial Arts.

Zen in the Martial Arts has achieved a prominent place, particularly in the art of the sword and archery. Technical skill in combat is worthless if it is not accompanied by an inner tranquility, by a vigilant spirit that does not stop anywhere.

As the Zen monk Takuan said (1573-1645) "The true spirit is like *water* and the broken spirit is like ice", that is when the spirit stops on something, like ice on a branch, is bound and unarmed, when it is like water, there are thousands of possibilities and roads.

With the practice of Zen we arrive at the dimension of "exploded time", that is, in a dimension in which events are something detached and seem to be filmed in slow motion.

In combat the most ancestral instincts emerge, the deepest part of our being, and Zen through meditation allows the subconscious to rise to the surface. In this way one gets in touch with oneself and gets in tune first with one's own spritito, and then with the universe and consequently with the adversary. Perhaps with this Haiku that follows you will be able to help you understand this concept:

> *The water of the Hirosawa pond*
> *Doesn't think about reflecting the moon,*
> *nor, for its part, does the moon try to be*
> *reflected on the water.*

That is, there is only one moon in the sky, but the surface of each river reflects a moon. If there is no water, the moon will not be reflected, but water does not create the light of the moon. The moonlight does not change if it is reflected by many rivers, nor does it change its size.

Our spirit does not have to worry about the things on which it rests, just as things do not have to notice the presence of our spirit (http://www.rico54.com/zen/).

[52] The art of sushi preparation is an authentic Zen ceremony where the aesthetics of the composition and the preamble necessary for the pleasure of tasting.
(http://espresso.repubblica.it/food/dettaglio/lo-zen-e-larte-di-preparare-il-sushi/2061793.html).

[53] Spread over the centuries from India to China to Japan and then throughout Asia, it arrived in Europe, in France, through Master Taisen Deshimaru in 1967 and is now practiced and known throughout the world. (http://www.zenroma.it/zen/)

[54] http://www.zenroma.it/zen/

[55] Cf note 1.

[56] Citation of the refrain of the song "Holly and Benji" by the Gem Boys.

[57] Cf the book by Eugen Herrigel, "Zen and archery", ed.cit. (cfr. note 1)

[58] If you don't like the soccer-zen combination or it doesn't convince you, here is a golf-zen one , also inspired by the book

"Zen and archery".https://www.caneogolf.it/psicologia-del-golf/zen-e-golf/

[59] http://www.centodieci.it/2018/04/come-essere-piucreativi-con-lo-zen/

[60] https://www.visioneolistica.it/contadino-saggio-storie-zen/

[61] http://www.centodieci.it/2018/04/come-essere-piucreativi-con-lo-zen/

Meditation
for Beginners:

*THE MOST LIFE-CHANGING BOOK ON
TRANSCENDENTAL MEDITATION THAT
WILL SHAPE YOUR THINKING ON HOW
TO MEDITATE IN PRACTICAL WAYS*

by

Gregory F. George

Introduction to Meditation

The growing interest in meditation is an undoubtedly evidence of a need that has to be understood.

It is true, sadly, that meditation is considered, by those who settle for superficial definitions, a "form of prayer".

Over the centuries, there has been a constant progress of the human consciousness and an ever increasing awareness of the nature and the world in which the man lives.

The english word "meditation", that is translated mostly as a process of "reflection", does not seize the essence of the concept.

Meditate means make the mind completely receptive of the reality and clear up the thought processes.

Practically, meditation is the exercise of focusing the mind on one or more objects, images of thoughts (in some techniques not one of those) for religious, spiritual, philosophical purposes or simply to improve your own psychophysical conditions.

In the humanistic psychology sphere it is defined as a conscience state that can be reached through the voluntary addressing of our focus towards a given object (reflective meditation) or through the complete absence of thoughts (receptive meditation).

Receptive meditation is distinctive of many eastern philosophies and religions and its purpose if the absence of thoughts to allow the mind to reach a level of "awareness without thoughts".

In the reflective meditation, much closer to the western culture, instead the object of meditation can be anything. In practice, generally, are used displays of objects that concern the inner world as emotions or quality, or simply physical objects (images, sacred texts, etc.).

We could say that the goal of meditation is the contact with the soul until the union with it. Thus, the whole purpose of meditation is to enable the man to become in his own external display what he is in his inner reality. Through the practice of meditation the can identify himself with the soul aspect and not only with the personality traits.

By meditation, then, you can develop the soul skills. Every vehicle through which the soul express itself (on the mental, emotional and physical levels) brings innate hidden powers, but the soul, that is their origin, owns them in their purest form.

In our evolution, we arrived to understand the laws that operate in the natural world and some of the ones that rules the psychic world. We still have to discover and use scientifically the ones of the spiritual kingdom. Meditation draws near this discovery.

In the preliminary stages of meditation a lot of resolution and perseverance are needed.

The first step in this discipline, that is the concentration, sometimes brings incredible results. Some people discover themselves; finding hidden skills and an understanding never used before; they develop an awareness of the phenomenal world that appears extraordinary to them; they detect unexpectedly the reality of the mind and the possibility to use it, and they understand clearly the distinction between the connoisseur and the instrument of knowledge.

At the same time, however, they feel that something is missing. The previous dreams of fulfillment and peace that prayers and mystic meditation made possible disappear and they experience temporally a feeling of dryness, of emptiness, of defect that is often very pathetic. This is provoked by the fact that the center of attention distanced itself from everything that is connected to the senses.

What the mind knows and can remember is not very clear yet, and the sentient apparate does not impose itself in the usual way to the conscience. It is a transitioning period, that we must bear until the new world starts impressing.

One of the first effects of the meditation is usually an increasing of efficiency in the daily lifestyle, both if it happens at home, at the office or in any field of the human activity. The mental application to the ordinary occupations is already, in itself, a concentration exercise with impressive results. Indeed, even if we do not reach the final revelation through the practice of meditation and concentration, we would still have learned a lot and our life would be enriched; the productivity would be surely bigger and the influence sphere would be wider.

Short story about Meditation

Usually associated to Eastern doctrine, meditation is a common element to the majority of religions and it is integral part of the monotheist cultures.

Between Christians and Muslims, for example, it is considered a form of prayer thanks to which the observants get closer to God, focusing on themselves and on other people. But meditation, as a part shared by many religions, has also a concrete proof, that goes beyond spirituality. Just think of prayer necklaces: the rosary for Christians, the japa mala for Induists, the juzu for Buddhists and the mishbaha for Muslims.

Fréderic Rosenfeld is the author of a long and interesting article published in the Mente & Cervello (Mind & Brain) section of the magazine Le Scienze, n.97 – January 2013, monthly publication about psychology and neuroscience.

In the article, he says that the term "meditate" has different meanings. In the common sense it means "reflect on something", "think about something". At the beginning of the XV century it meaned "reflect on a religious mystery".

The origin of the word can lead back to the latin words "meditari" and "mederi" that mean "cure, take care", sign that the connection between meditative practice and therapeutic effect on the physical, psychological, mental and spiritual plane was clear to the ancient people.

The practice of meditation has a really ancient history. The different meditation traditions find their genesis in philosophical or religious movement, still today known and spread even in the western world.

Taoism – "Tao" is a difficult word to translate because it contains many different meanings in regard of the different origins, times and places. It can be interpreted as "way, path, direction", and it indicates the spontaneous and natural flow of things, representing a structure that organizes the whole universe and in which the Qi makes its energetic principle circulate.

Taoism is a movement of thought that goes back probably to before 2000 b.C.. It unifies different mystical, philosophical and scientific movements. This "multiform" trait allowed it to survive through many centuries by adapting to other philosophical-religious movements, like Buddhism. In its original spirit, Taoism inspired the principles of chinese medicine, of the management of politics, of cosmology and of soothsaying, as well as different meditative practices like Tai Chi Chuan, Qi Gong, Do In, Chinese and Japanese martial arts.

91

In the Tao-te-king, one the most important work of Taoism, it is referred to the existence of a unique, invisible, untouchable precept, from which the multiplicity of creation appears.

Currently are used many meditative practices inspired by Tao, the common goal is the work on Qi to promote the circulation of this inner breath. Some taoist meditations require to the practicing to develop in their minds the equivalent of Shamatha, a state of inner calm. These are the practices developed in the so-called "North school". In the so-called "South school", instead, you are encouraged to commit to the centers connected to the Qi circulation in the organism, namely on the breath. But in Taoism, the boundary between body and mind remains very faded. Some practices, then, require a seated and static posture; others provide for sweet and repeated motions.

Buddhism – It is born in VI century D.C. in the north part of India, inspired by the historical figure of the prince Siddharta Gautama. According to sources, he got to know the external world after a long youth spent inside the royal palace, that protected him from the sufferings that trouble the mankind and that allowed him to devote himself to the earthly pleasures. However, after becoming aware of suffering, of diseases, of misery and of despair of mankind, he was appalled by them and escaped from his palace. Close to Benares, after a long meditation, he drew inspiration for his "for noble truths" on the origin and on the remedies against suffering.

Thus, initially, Buddhism intends only to fix the human pain by practicing simple and universal rules to reach a better knowledge of Ego. Therefore, some branches of Buddhism deified the man Siddharta and his message. And, indeed, through buddhist meditation, the practicing can reach the same experience that can be felt in the union with divine, that is perceiving the effects of a mystical union, of a cosmic unifier principle and of compassion towards any being.

Buddhist meditation techniques are very different between the various movements (so-called Theravada, Mahayana, Vajrayana schools) and the various geographical locations (Thailand, Myanmar, Japan, China, Tibet, Vietnam). The common elements concern Shamantha and Vipassana, but they differ on the ways to realize them. For example, the importance given to posture is variable: in the zen Japanese school is an essential element of the practice; other schools, like the Indo-Burmese Vipassana, are more flexible. Some schools more encourage a meditative moving practice: walking in the full awareness of Vipassana, Kinhin of Zen Soto, or even in unusual conditions, like under a waterfall, in the Japanese Takigyo.

Over time the various methods merge or differ, according to the kind of mind that their practice develops: for example the practice of Tibetan Shiné is close to the Indo-Burmese one of Anapa because both of them focus their attention on breathing. Similarly the Tibetan Demis med snying rje meditation is close to the Indo-Burmese Metta bhavan practice because both of them result in compassion and unconditional love towards sentient beings. Even the Tibetan Ton glen aspire to compassion by activating significantly the creative imagination: here the practicing imagines to inhale the neighbor's pain in the form of a steam that vanishes inside himself and gives rise to a radiant and noble light that releases with every breath. Kyan, finally, in Buddhist Japan, is a powerful support for meditation, through Koan zen that the master submits to the pupil and that push the latter to break the mold of rationality to head towards the spiritual awakening (Satori).

Induism – It is a conceptual universe rich and varied in its origins, that characterizes the philosophical, moral, theological, scientific and cosmological fields of Indian subcontinent. Like Taoism, it is a constellation of cultural movements more than a strict set of beliefs.

In centuries, Induism has blossomed in different systems and philosophical schools: among them there is Yoga, that proposed harmony and reunification of

94

the body-mind sent through body and hands positions and breathing techniques. In the Yoga philosophy, Prana has a central role: it is a concept similar to the Chinese Qi, an energy that pervades the cosmos but circulates also in the physical body thanks to the Yoga practice. Yoga, however, even if comes out the Induism cradle, does not take from it the dogmatic, religious or doctrinaire aspects.

Born for religion, meditation has spread in the western secularized world as a relaxing technique. Practices like Yoga or Mantras are appreciated not only for the psychological benefits, but as well for the positive effects they have on health.

Beyond the impressive mystical-religious background, there is a wide offer of, so to speak, secular techniques, most notably the "Transcendental Meditation", a registered trademark, introduced in 1958 by Maharishi Mahesh Yogi and widespread all over the world, but mostly in USA, with his encoded seven steps program.

Kabat-Zinn, american doctor, and founder of the Stress Reduction Clique in the University of Massachusetts, pushed himself to transform this ancient practice into a protocol, declaring that "you only need eight weeks to learn to put to rest the cardiovascular system, rebalance the nervous system and allow the immune system to express its own potential".

According to a study promoted by Harvard University, in fact, meditation could induce physical and biochemical changes in the organism, and it is now established that the relaxation, for example, that follows transcendental meditation can affect metabolism, heart rhythm, blood pressure and breathing..

Very popular is the Vipassana Meditation, of Buddhist origin, developed by Burmese and Thai monks a century before, it is proposed, as well in many Italian centers, in ten days courses.

Undoubtedly there is a Meditation marketing, like, for example, the online propositions of the guru Osho Rajneesh (1931-1990), with a catalogue that offers techniques for all tastes – from the dynamic practice to kundalini, from the dancing technique (nataraj) to the nocturnal one (gourishankar).

However, despite the cultural and historical origins that definite it, it is possible to find constant elements that are common to the majority of meditative techniques.

Generally, in the meditative practice, we can reckon two fundamental elements.

The first element is "Shamatha", a term that means "calm, peaceful" and that indicates how Meditation brings a remarkable and long mental calm. The Meditation act, actually, can bring to the appearance of dramatic moments like excesses of anguish, the resurfacing of painful emotions, an increased heart rate. However, these tormented moments stay isolated, because Shamatha involve a state of serene background that continues beyond the times of Meditation and involves the constant relationship between oneself and the external world. Shamatha is not a technique by itself, but it is possible to reach this state through various techniques, each one of those invites to concentrate on a precise object: breathing, the contemplation of a flame, the color of an object or a mental image.

The second common element to the majority of meditative practices is Vipassana or "clear vision, conscious attention". Vipassana allows us to perceive things as they are, and this is possible only thanks to a mind free from its own convictions and from schemes born from its own fears. Moreover, Vipassana is the technique to enter in a clearer knowledge of their own deepest being, the psychic, sensible and emotional world that rules over our behavior in an almost oblivious way.

The word "Vipassana" indicated a precise meditative technique of Indo-Burmese inspiration, whose origin had been rediscovered by Buddha. You need to focus an assiduous and detached attention to corporeal sensations that arise, evolve and disappear, moment by moment, on the body surface or in the bowels. To reach this attention is needed a regular and dedicated practice. Vipassana allows who practices it constantly to develop the mental quality of equanimity, that is the mood consistency, the detachment and the serenity in front of superficial things and phenomena.

It is possible to practice Zazen (zen Buddhism meditation) or Hatha Yoga or following Buddha's paths without losing your own faith, whatever it may be: Christian, Muslim or Jewish religion. Meditative practices harmonize with the practicing's faith, they even strengthen and support it. The meditative experience can bring the practicing to perceive a compassionate love towards every being.

In the case of Buddhism, nothing evokes the existence of an highest being or of a transcendence, in fact, in some original messages it is proposed to remedy to human sufferings through the practice of some simple universal rules that are absolutely independent from any religious intent. Therefore, in order to practice Meditation, it is not necessary to have a belief, neither to not have it, so it can adapt to the modern man need, him being secular or religious.

About the goal of Meditation there is not a lot to say: actually, Meditation does not have to serve anything, in fact, meditate implies to not expect any effect and to not foreshadow anything. The meditator behavior is of not having any intention, it is an acting without acting. However, in the same philosophical-religious traditions in which meditative practices have their origins, the healing principles are clearly expressed: the Chinese Qi inspired the Traditional Chinese Medicine, and Buddha searched remedy for the pain of his human brothers through his "four noble truths"; at the same time, the Induist Prana, or vital energy, communicated its breath of life to Yoga. This is because the meditative techniques, like it is known from centuries, play a beneficial activity on body and mind.

In the Western world, from several years, we rely on the therapeutic effect of meditative practices. Various international researches, through the measurement of physiological parameters, neuro-images, EEG, electrocardiogram and statistical surveys, confirm the benefits of Meditation. This union between western science and the conscience of spiritual traditions creates conditions that enrich both of them. Following this line, it has been created, at the end of the Eighties, the Mind and Life Institute, that has proposed to promote the dialogue between Buddhism and scientists open to Meditation, to encourage the exchange between these two worlds, through scientific studies that bring closer meditators of different schools and specialists of mind and health.

Types of Meditation

Dynamic Meditation, Vipassana, Zazen, Samatha, Mindfulness, Transcendental Meditation, these are all names of some types of Meditation (some of them are copyrighted).

Let's try to know them better.

Dynamic Meditation is a meditation invented by Osho.

Is it a Meditation that you practice while dancing, screaming, moving and waving your arms and at some point you stop and bring your attention to what you were doing in the moment you stopped.

It is a challenging Meditation; you do in a group of people, and, probably, Osho thought it for us, western people.

Vipassana Meditation (in the ancient Hindi language Pali means "see things deeply, how they really are") is one of the most ancient techniques of Meditation in India. It has been rediscovered and teached by the Buddha Gotama more than 2500 years ago like an universal method to escape from every kind of suffering. It is an universal technique, it can be practiced by everyone, defined as Art of Living. This non-sectarian Meditation points to the complete elimination of mental impurities and to the resultant greatest happiness of the full liberation.

Vipassana is a way of self-transformation through self-observation. It focuses on the deep interconnection between mind and body, which can be experienced directly by disciplined attention to the physical sensations that form the life of the body, and that continuously interconnect and condition the life of the mind. It is this observation-based, self-exploratory journey to the common root of mind and body that dissolves mental impurity, resulting in a balanced mind full of love and compassion.

The scientific laws that operates one's thoughts, feelings, judgements and sensations become clear. Through direct experience, the nature of how one grows or regresses, how one produces suffering or frees oneself from suffering is understood. Life become characterized by increased awareness, non-delusion, self-control and peace.

Zazen Meditation

Unlikely, Vipassana Meditation, in which the posture is relatively free, the zen Meditation is practiced in the lotus position, in the half-lotus position or simply with crossed legs, seated on the zafu, that is much more than a simple pillow. The posture is a fundamental part of this technique, and the fifth lumbar vertebra is the keystore of posture. Pushing it in front it aligns perfectly with the spine. Only starting from this moment one can start to meditate, eyes open, contemplating the wall in front of him. The word Zazen, "simply seated", means that we seat in meditation with simplicity, without goals or expectation, not wanting or thinking anything, even without the idea of being seated like that. The secret and the difficulty stay exactly in this word: simply. When we Zazen seat, indeed, we lose wisdom and knowledge and we enter in the practice of not-knowing. Entering in the non-knowledge allows us to not having detachment between us and our self, to adhere to everything and not to something in particular.

Samatha Meditation is a type of Buddhist meditation with Hindu origin. It is based on the consciousness of breathing, through the prolonged observation (at least 15-30 minutes) of the phased of inhaling and exhaling in one of the points where the sensation of the breath in that circulates in the body is clearer: at the entrance of the nose, in the stomach or on the solar plexus. The aim of this method it to reach a dimension of inner peace, and it is propaedeutic to Vipassana Meditation.

Mindfulness Meditation

Mindfulness is a training based on specific exercises that involve body and attention, which final goal is to grow the habit to awareness to reach a mental stare more inclined to satisfaction and happiness.

In 1979 Kabat-Zinn, molecular biologist with a long meditative practice behind, while preparing the base concepts of Transcendental Meditation, realized a protocol that arrived to University of Massachussets Medical Center, paving the way for the practice of Mindfulness, that rotates around the two fundamental concepts of awareness and concentration.

Awareness is nothing more than the ability to act as much as possible in an intentional way, throwing an accurate but not judgmental look to anything you do, you say, you think.

Concentration is the positive effort of mind that trains to lead the attention towards its object in a pure way, without the thought interference that suffers from the past experience or from the projections on the future.

Mindfulness is nothing more than mental presence. It means being aware of what we are doing, of what we are living, at any moment. During the MBSR (Mindfulness Based Stress Reduction) protocol are proposed many styles of formal meditation, among them anyone can find what suits him best, but the most important trait of this practice is always the mental presence in the daily act and deeds.

This technique, originally applied to anxiety and chronical pain researches, proved through clinical evidence benefits in the treatment of generalized stress, depression, substance abuse, chronical pain, disease, disturbance in attention and learning.

Transcendental Meditation draws from the vedic tradition, thus from the Indian tradition, and it has been brought in the western world by Maharishi, who has its copyright.

We owe to Transcendental Meditation the fact that there have been many scientific studies on the general benefits of Meditation. This scientific research continues still today with Mindfulness.

Transcendental Meditation became really famous because it is considered the rich people Meditation. Among them, we can recall the Beatles.

It is a Meditation that you do with a mantra. The Sanskrit word "mantra" comes from "manas" (mind or thinking principle) and "tra" (what protects and brings over). The inner listening of a mantra, a chosen word, a phrase or a subtle sound keeps attention directed to a point, protecting it from being unduly influenced by emotion, thoughts and moods, bringing it over confused or foggy mental states, until it reaches a super- conscientious clear level. In Transcendental Meditation the Mantra is secret; so, being it a copyright, nobody, except the Master, can start its practice. Even though the mantras are public, that is everyone can know the mantras, the Master assigns the personal Mantra, that is unique and it cannot be shared.

Meditation is therefore a practice that has its own techniques and rules. Meditating without a technique or outside the rules laid down by the various types of Meditation is equivalent to thinking. That is, the contrary of what Meditation is. When we think we are subjected to thoughts. When we meditate we get far away from thoughts, we observe them and we do not let ourselves be conditioned.

Outside the various Meditation techniques there are other practices (that are often called meditative), like for example self-hypnosis, autogenic training, mental programming, etc., that produce different effects, as different are the reasons to practice them.

For example, the **Metta practice**, loving kindness meditation, is a meditative technique whose aim is to develop compassion.

Its roots lie in the Buddhist tradition, but it can be adopted and practiced by anyone, independently from his beliefs. Loving kindness meditation is essentially a vehicle to manage to grow love and kindness in the purest and most unselfish way possible. The benevolence practice (the one of the opening of the heart) is a practice that creates suggestions.

Thus it is not an awareness technique, but it is a technique that promotes suggestions.

Through Meditation it is possible to control our own mind, to live a balanced life and to find happiness in our self, getting over the fact that are others (people or events) that make us happy.

All types of Meditation use instruments to get what they repropose. The instruments of Meditation pass through senses: for example, hearing (Mantra) or sight (images).

Meditation on a Mantra or on a Passage

It is a question of repeating, mentally or aloud, a word, a sentence, a passage, a prayer. By concentrating the mind on this positive message, it is freed from negative thoughts and is "reprogrammed". The word mantra is a very ancient term, which means vehicle of thought.

This word is born from the union of two terms, that are MAN and TRA.

The word MAN that means "to think".

The word TRA that means "to act".

Basically mantras are divided into two categories: personal mantras and impersonal mantras. The former is generally invocations of a divinity or divine being, while the latter are formulas that do not refer to an entity but to an illuminating truth or a concept that is generally more abstract.

The most common mantra is undoubtedly the **OM**, the invocation of our divine aspect. It's what you've seen and heard acting in cinemas and that, thanks to the new-age philosophy, has spread more widely. All you have to do is try: keep your back straight, your eyes closed and well focused on your breath, we begin to mentally repeat this word for about ten minutes. In case of external distractions, reciting the mantra helps to regain the balance of the breath and to welcome the peace that goes with it.

"**I am Buddha**" is another very effective mantra, to be recited with the knowledge that, in this case, Buddha is the highest part of us as enlightened beings.

"**I am one**" is instead an alternative that has more or less the same efficacy, but it allows us to come into profound contact with ourselves: we affirm our Ego in the here and now, letting it vibrate.

Meditation on an object or on an image

Whether it is the flame of a candle, a crucifix or a mandala, the principle is similar to that of the mantra: we focus our attention on a positive image, in order to absorb the qualities of the object of our contemplation or, simply, to let each thought "evaporate".

Meditating is a commitment that requires perseverance and willpower. It is certainly worth it but this is discovered only after a certain period. To begin with, therefore, it is better to make it easier, to reduce the risk of "giving up" too soon. Some techniques (such as Meditation on a mantra or on the flame of a candle) can also be practiced alone. Others (such as Vipassana's retreat or Zazen's session) require, at least initially, the presence of a master.

Start with the technique that seems easier to implement, easier to insert in your days, and carry it out daily for at least two or three months. At this point you will certainly want to learn more and you can find out about other options and centers that offer them.

Transcendental Meditation

Transcendental Meditation is easy because it is fundamentally different from other meditation techniques. As we have seen, most people believe that "meditation" is a form of mind control, achieved by some kind of concentration (a sound, breath, or trying to maintain awareness of the present moment), with the goal of achieving a certain silence or relaxation. Concentration, however, requires rigorous training, and is usually not so pleasant. What is proved is that controlling the mind is unnatural.

The Transcendental Meditation technique was rediscovered by Maharishi Mahesh Yogi, under the guidance of his master. He has thus restored correctness in the practice of true meditation, which does not consist at all in controlling the mind. And he developed a method to train people to activate a natural process by which the mind reaches, by itself, a state of complete inner silence, absolutely without effort.

Introduced in the western world in 1955, Transcendental Meditation is inspired by an Indian spiritual tradition. Maharishi thus embodies the awakening of Indian meditation and traditions.

109

We are talking about six million people who had been taught this technique in the world. A number that, despite the small controversies, is still emblematic of a certain charm and, above all, of the desire to be happy.

First of all, Meditation comes from the aspiration to be self-aware, to understand what is happening inside us or to fight stress and depression. Goals identify Transcendental Meditation as the bearer of significant physical benefits.

Maharishi Mahesch Yogi (literally: Great Seer, Great Lord and Divine) is the man who introduced Transcendental Meditation (also called TM). Born in 1917 and died in 2008, he became a symbol of the American counterculture and his image had been mad popular by the Times who dedicated several covers to him.

A success linked to the ease of the technique, which, as we have already seen, is, and has been, very fashionable among some stars. While his critics associate his technique with the name of "cult", Maharishi establishes a university, schools and colleges in different countries.

In absolute terms, most practitioners agree that Transcendental Meditation reduces stress, improving the quality of sleep and reducing fatigue.

Refocusing day after day, freeing oneself from what is happening, making the brain more attentive, having greater self-awareness, in short, daily practice has shown that Transcendental Meditation improves pleasantly the quality of life.

In this meditation, we do not concentrate, we are not trying to control the mind, but we let the mind follow its natural instinct to achieve a greater happiness. In other words, it goes inward and acquires the consciousness of the bliss in Being.

The practice of Transcendental Meditation is, according to Maharishi, the ability to develop a state of awakening at rest, which would result in a release of tensions and anxiety. An awareness of self that, day by day, would promote the management of stress, making us more attentive to what is happening.

There is also talk of a reduction in high blood pressure or of a significant reduction in stress. It would also revitalize the body and improve the nervous system. A complete discipline, which would therefore improve well-being from a general point of view.

This is therefore the principle and the message conveyed by Transcendental Meditation: a daily practice that favors general psychophysical well-being.

Summarizing, thus, Transcendental Meditation would allow to:

-reduce anxiety,

-meditate without effort,

-become aware of oneself and of one's body,

-stick to a daily practice,

-solve or reduce many potential physical problems.

However, Transcendental Meditation is a particular type of meditation that can be practiced in the presence of a teacher.

This is the person who has the role of instructor, initiator, guide to discover TM. A crucial role, considering the fact that for many people the practice of meditation is a real tool for personal development.

Transcendental Meditation is therefore a technique of relaxation and personal development slightly different from the others. In fact, here, there is no need for effort or concentration. It suffices a small preparatory training and the will to practice daily.

The practice is based on a conscious inner peace of one's body, simply by paying attention to a mantra that has to be recited in silence. A mantra that will be evoked individually by the teacher and that can be a word or even an idea.

The principle is therefore to repeat this mantra according to the teachings of the master. However, this same teacher must be trained by the Maharashi Mahesh Yogi organization.

The training of teachers takes place in the form of lectures, personal interviews, supported by a six-month follow-up.

The role of the teacher is therefore very important, if not fundamental. However it is the weak point of the discipline, since learning how to meditate with a teacher is essential.

This is undoubtedly a message a little more advanced than the awareness Meditation or the Zen meditation, almost a claim, which some do not hesitate to reconnect to a sectarian type model.

The teacher's guide, besides being indispensable, requires a real involvement, a real desire to train, to take courses and has a financial cost. A point that can be perceived as negative, since meditation is a discipline that generally does not require any material, no course, only our body and our mind.

Therefore it is not a meditative practice like the others, in which the lessons are given in a free and random way. In this case, training is considered necessary for the correct functioning of spirituality.

A sort of guided meditation, in which personal development and this state of letting go are accessible only through a specific process.

And this, perhaps, may be intended like a limit of Transcendental Meditation.

In fact, it has often been perceived through the media precisely because of the need to learn, not as a potential training from which to benefit through its practice, but as a relaxation discipline of its own, linked to the present moment.

The reason is simple and is in particular due to the great media exposure of the founder of Transcendental Meditation. In fact, while Maharishi Mahesh Yogi from the 1960s surrounded himself with stars like Stevie Wonder, Hugh Jackman or Oprah Winfrey, the regular TM practice became very popular.

Invited to several American television programs, he actually helped to democratize Transcendental Meditation, but opened the way to various controversies, such as that concerning the sectarian nature of the discipline.

Everything has been said about Transcendental Meditation. It has been given a religious, political and sometimes financial dimension. The fact remains that it stands as a branch of meditation which, although it does not satisfy everyone, has the merit of being talked about.

How Transcendental Meditation works

The human being is a set of numerous different elements, chakras with relative rupas or bodies, which in most traditions are seven but in others they have a variable number up to twenty. Each yoga is based on one of these elements of the human being, focusing on it and using it as a launching pad to enter into union (yoga - unite) with a divine correspondent of the element that composes us. Speaking in general terms the human being seems able to experience and realize the great divine experiences:

-the immanent Divine, that is the individual soul;

-the cosmic Divine, that is the universal soul;

-the absolute Divine, Purushottama, that is the transcendence above time, space, cosmos and individuality.

It is towards this experience that some yogas aim straight, not spending energy or time in the search for the Divine in the individual or for the Divine in the cosmos as a relative, multiple and characterized manifestation.

These two forms of divine experiences are reflections of the transcendence in a phenomenon, cosmos or individual soul, which can only draw fragmented and incomplete gleams, therefore not transcendental, due to the fact that the cosmos and every single element are linked to time, to space and dualities. In the most extreme cases, researchers of transcendence consider the cosmic manifestation a dream, a lie or an ill-fated illusion from which one comes out entering a constant union (yoga) with transcendence, taking into account the impossibility of describing it or representing it.

According to the Hindu tradition at the origin of the cosmic manifestation there was a sound, a mantra, AUM; just as in the Gospels we are told that "In the beginning was the Word", that "The verb was God", and that "everything was done through him".

The most modern researches, with radio telescopes and quantum microscopes, tell us that matter and energy are two different versions of the same reality, made up of vibrations and frequencies, that is sounds. Sound therefore seems to be the only element that can be reported by the transcendent planes in those of relative reality, made of matter, energy, life, mind.

According to the method of Maharishi Mahesh Yogi the practice of some mantras for about twenty minutes a day would free from anxiety and lead to the so-called self-realization. The journal Science also became interested in the effects of the practice of mantra-based Transcendental Meditation, apparently finding general health benefits. Following this, even decades after the Beatles experience, there are many followers and practitioners, even famous ones, including the brilliant director David Lynch, who benefit from the practice of mantra-based Transcendental Meditation. Today "Transcendental Meditation" is a registered trademark, there are certified instructors able to give mantras to practitioners and there are real curricula and training courses, programs and a foundation.

Benefits of Transcendental Meditation

During the practice of Transcendental Meditation the body almost immediately reaches a state of rest much deeper even than the rest we get during our deepest sleep, a condition that we usually only reach after a few hours of sleep. This deep rest allows the body to remove even the most deeply rooted stresses. We are able to heal ourselves much more than we think. All we have to do is just activate our inner healing power.

The effects of the self-healing process that we can activate with Transcendental Meditation are more evident in those who need it the most.

Stress is the main cause of 90% of all diseases. Teaching people how to remove their own stress essentially means teaching them how to prevent disease. This is why many doctors today recommend Transcendental Meditation to their patients.

The practice of Transcendental Meditation is not limited to improving our health and well-being, but it also improves the functioning of our brain, thereby creating:

-more emotional stability

-more self confidence

-more energy

-better interpersonal relationships

-improvement of creativity and intelligence

-improvement of memory and concentration

Many people, it is true, continue to affirm that meditation has no scientific basis and is only a discipline for its own sake, and though experts and meditation teachers want to try to clarify how wrong this line of thinking is, they are often asked scientific evidence to support their explanations.

It must be said that there are over three thousand scientific studies on the benefits of meditation.

These studies are based on different types of meditation. Some effects, such as the increased compassion and sociality, are more evident following specific meditation techniques (such as loving kindness, which is a Buddhist meditation). However, in general, any type of authentic meditation includes the majority of these benefits in one way or another.

Some of the studies have indicated that practicing TM even just for twenty minutes every day for a couple of weeks is already enough to start experiencing the benefits.

We cite the sources that report some of the researches carried out on the results obtained.

1. Brain and mood

Transcendental Meditation attenuates and fights depression

In a study conducted in five middle schools in Belgium that involved around 400 students aged between 13 and 20, Professor Filip Raes concluded that "students taking Mindfulness lessons in school hours show a smaller tendency towards depression, anxiety and stress up to six months later. Furthermore, these students were less likely to develop marked symptoms of depression."

Another study, conducted by the University of California on a sample of patients who suffered from depression in the past, concluded that meditation significantly decreases mental rumination and dysfunctional thoughts.

A final study concludes that meditation can be effective in treating depression to an extent similar to an antidepressant therapy.

Sources: ScienceDaily, Link Springer, Jama Network

Transcendental Meditation helps fight post-natal depression

Pregnant women who took part in a ten-week training course experienced a significant reduction in depressive symptoms, according to a pilot study carried out by the University of Michigan. Future mothers also showed a more intense bond with the children they were carrying. The results have been published in "Complementary therapies in clinical practice".

Source: Medical News Today

Praticing Transcendental Meditation regolates mood disorders and reduces anxiety

This is the conclusion of over twenty controlled studies detected from the databases of PubMed, PsycInfo, and Cochrane, involving meditation techniques, meditative prayer, yoga and relaxation response.

Another research concludes that Meditation can be effective in treating anxiety at a similar level to antidepressant therapy.

Sources: The Journal of Alternative and Complementary Medicine, Jama Network

Transcendental Meditation reduces stress and general anxiety

A study conducted in the University of Wisconsin-Madison noted how "Open monitoring" Meditation practices reduce the density of gray matter in areas of the brain related to anxiety and stress. Those who meditated were able to "follow moment by moment the flow of stimulations to which the group was subjected and showed a less inclination to 'remain blocked' on any stimulation."

Open monitoring meditation involves the non-reactive monitoring of the meditation experience moment by moment, and is mainly used as a way to recognize the nature of emotional and cognitive models.

Transcendental Meditation helps reduce the symptoms of panic attacks

In a study published in the Journal of Psychiatry, twenty-two patients who had been diagnosed with anxiety disorder or panic disorder underwent three months of meditation and relaxation training. As a result, for twenty of these patients the effects of panic and anxiety have been substantially reduced, and the benefits have persisted over time as confirmed by subsequent follow-up visits.

Transcendental Meditation increases the density of grey matter in the brain

A group of Harvard neuro scientists conducted an experiment during which sixteen individuals underwent an eight-week course, through guided meditations and integration of awareness into their daily activities. The results were reported by Dr. Sara Lazar. At the end of the experiment, magnetic resonances showed an increase in the concentration of grey matter in the brain areas involved in learning and memory, and in those that regulate emotions, the sense of self and perspective.

Other studies, similarly, show an increase in grey matter in the hippocampus and frontal lobe in people who meditate regularly.

Sources: Psychiatry Research Neuroimaging, ScienceDirect

Transcendental Meditation significantly improves psychomotor vigilance and can reduce the need for sleep

In a research conducted by the University of Kentucky, participants were tested on four different conditions: control (C), sleep (N), meditation (M) and sleep deprivation with meditation. Both non-meditators, novice meditators and expert meditators took part in the experiment. The results suggest that:

meditation provides an improvement in short-term performance, even in beginner meditators. For more experienced meditators, more hours spent in meditation are associated with a significant decrease in total sleep time when compared to individuals of the same sex and age who do not practice meditation. Whether or not meditation can effectively replace a portion of sleep or a sleep debt is still a matter of further investigation.

Sources: NCBI, DoctorsOnTM, Time Magazine

Transcendental Meditation in the long term improves the ability to generate gamma waves in the brain

In a study conducted by neuroscientist Richard Davidson of the University of Wisconsin that involved a group of Tibetan Buddhist monks along with beginning meditators, it was found that inexperienced meditators "showed a slight increase in gamma activity, but most part of the monks showed huge increases never seen before in the neuroscientific literature ".

Source: The Wall Street Journal

Transcendental Meditation helps reduce alcoholism and drug addiction

Three studies on meditation conducted on a group of prisoners suggested that this practice can help reduce alcohol and drug abuse.

Source: Journal Of Alternative and Complementary Medicine

2. Concentration and skills

Transcendental Meditation improves concentration, attention and the ability to work under stress

A study conducted by Katherine MacLean of the University of California noted that during and after a meditation session the subjects subjected to it were more likely to keep the attention span high, particularly on repetitive and boring activities.

Another study proved that, even with only twenty minutes a day of practice, students were able to improve their performance in cognitive ability tests, in some cases with results even ten times better than in the non-meditating group. Similar results were also observed in the performance of tasks that required information processing and were designed to induce imminent deadline stress.

The experiment showed that the meditators had a thicker prefrontal cortex, concluding that meditation could compensate for the loss of cognitive abilities that comes with old age.

Sources: Time Magazine, NCBI, Link Springer

Transcendental Meditation improves information processing and decision making

Eileen Luders, an assistant professor at the UCLA Neuro Imaging Laboratory, discovered with some colleagues that long-term meditators possess large amounts of gyration ("bending" of the cerebral cortex, which can allow the brain to process the information more quickly) compared to people who do not meditate. Scientists suspect that gyration is responsible for a better processing of information, of decision-making capacity, of memory formation and of improved attention.

Source: UCLA Newsroom

Transcendental Meditation increases mental strength, resilience and emotional intelligence

Psychotherapist Dr. Ron Alexander reports in his book "Wise Mind, Open Mind" that the mind control process that occurs through meditation enhances mental strength, resilience and emotional intelligence.

Source: Dr. Ron Alexander

Transcendental Meditation makes you stronger in situations of pain

A research team at the University of Montreal exposed thirteen Zen masters and thirteen non-practitioners to the same degree of painful heat, measuring their brain activity in a functional magnetic resonance imaging (fMRI) scanner. They discovered that Zen meditation practitioners reported less pain. To be more precise, Zen masters reported less pain than their neurological output indicated by fMRI. In practice, even if their brains received the same amount of input, less pain was recorded in their mind.

Source: Time Magazine, NCBI, David Lynch Foundation

Transcendental Meditation mitigates pain better than morphine

In an experiment conducted by Wake Forest Baptist Medical Center, fifteen healthy volunteers, who were new to Meditation, participated to four twenty-minute lessons to learn it, focusing on the breath. Both before and after the meditation practice, the brain activity of study of the participants was examined using MRI, while pain was inflicted on them using heat.

This is the first study to show that even just over an hour of meditation can drastically reduce both the pain experience and the activation of pain-related areas of the brain. There was a 40% reduction in pain intensity and a 57% reduction in pain-related unpleasantness. Meditation has resulted in a reduction of the painful stimulations even higher than morphine or other pain-relieving drugs, which generally reduce pain by about 25%.

Source: Huffington Post

Transcendental Meditation helps manage attention deficit hyperactivity disorder (ADHD)
In a study of fifty patients with ADHD, the group that underwent MBCT (cognitive therapy based on Mindfulness) showed a reduced hyperactivity, a reduced impulsiveness and an increased capacity to act with awareness, contributing to a overall improvement in the symptoms of inattention.

Sources: Clinical Neurophysiology Journal, DoctorsOnTM

Transcendental Meditation increases the ability to stay focused despite distractions
A research conducted by Emory University in Atlanta showed that participants with more experience of Meditation show greater connectivity within the areas of the brain that control attention. These neural

relationships can be involved in the development of cognitive abilities, such as maintaining attention and breaking free from distraction. Moreover, the benefits of the practice in a normal state of consciousness during the day were also observed, maintaining the cognitive abilities outside the meditative sessions in daily life.

The practice of meditation was examined by focusing attention on breath.

Source: Frontiers Journal

Transcendental Meditation improves learning, memory and self-awareness
Practicing Meditation for a long time increases the density of the grey matter in the areas of the brain associated with learning, memory, self-awareness, compassion and introspection.

Source: NCBI

Transcendental Meditation improves memory
According to Catherine Kerr of the Martinos Center for Biomedical Diagnostics and the Osher Research Center, "meditation can improve many mental abilities, including the quick recall of memories".

Source: PsychCentral

Transcendental Meditation improves mood and psychological well-being

Researchers at Nottingham Trent University in United Kingdom found that, when a group of people with stress and depression problems underwent Meditation training, all participants experienced improvements in psychological well-being.

Source: Link Springer

Transcendental Meditation prevents from falling into the multitasking trap too often

Multitasking is not just a false myth of productivity, it is also a source of stress. Continuously changing focus is one of the most strenuous activities for the brain, and it induces feelings of distraction and dissatisfaction with the work done.

In a research conducted by the University of Washington and the University of Arizona, human resources personnel underwent eight weeks of training in both Meditation and body relaxation techniques, and participants performed a very stressful multitasking test, both before that after training. The group that practiced meditation reported lower stress levels and showed a better memory for the tasks they had done; they also jumped from task to task less often and remained focused on longer tasks.

Source: ACM Digital Library

Transcendental Meditation helps us distribute limited brain resources

When the brain is presented with two different objectives to watch out for, one after the other in a very short time (half a second difference), the second object is often ignored. This phenomenon is called "attentional-blink".

In an experiment conducted by the University of California, a stream of random letters in rapid succession was shown on a computer screen. For each session a white screen appeared randomly between one letter and another, and the participants were then asked, immediately after the end of the flow, to type in the numbers they had seen. It was also asked if they thought it was shown a blank screen.

The persons who had practiced the months of intense meditation showed they had better control over attention distribution and perception of resources. They also showed a lower allocation of brain resources for each letter shown, which resulted in the reduction of the attention-blink.

Source: PLOS Biology

Transcendental Meditation improve visual spatial processing and working memory
Research has proved that even after four meditation sessions the participants had significantly improved visuospatial processing, working memory and executive functions.

Source: ScienceDirect

Transcendental Meditation prepares us to better cope with stressful events
A study by the All India Institute of Medical Sciences, conducted on thirty-two adults who had never practiced Meditation before, showed that if Meditation is practiced before a stressful event the negative effects of stress are mitigated.

Source: The Journal of Alternative and Complementary Medicine

Transcendental Meditation increases the subconscious mind awareness
A study conducted by researchers at the University of Sussex in the UK has shown that people who practice meditation experience a more extended pause between unconscious impulses and action, and are also less subject to hypnosis.

Source: New Scientist

Transcendental Meditation stimulates creativity
Research from the University of Leiden (Netherlands) has shown that the practice of Open monitoring meditation (non-reactive monitoring of experience moment by moment) has positive effects on creativity and divergent thinking. The participants who had experienced Meditation showed better results in a task in which they were required to think creatively by proposing new ideas.

Source: The Journal of Alternative and Complementary Medicine

3. Body and health
Transcendental Meditation reduces the risk of heart diseases and stroke
Heart diseases claim more victims than any other disease.

In a study published at the end of 2012, a group of over two hundred high-risk individuals were asked to participate in a health education lesson that promoted exercise and a healthier diet, or to take part in a Transcendental Meditation course. Over the next 5 years the researchers who followed the progress of the participants found that those who attended the meditation course had a 48% reduction in their risk of heart attack, stroke and death.

Meditation has been found to have "significantly reduced the risk of mortality, myocardial infarction and stroke in patients with coronary artery disease. These changes have been associated with lower blood pressure and reduced psychosocial stress factors ".

Sources: Time Magazine, American Heart Association, HealthCentral

Transcendental Meditation affects the genes that control stress and immunity

A study by Harvard Medical School showed that, after practicing yoga and meditation, the individuals tested had improved the production, consumption and resistance of mitochondrial energy. This improvement develops the immune system and allows greater resistance to stress.

Sources: Journal of International Society of Psychoneuroendocrinology

Transcendental Meditation reduces blood pressure

Clinical research has shown that the practice of Zen meditation reduces stress and solves high blood pressure problems.

Another experiment, this time conducted with a technique called "relaxation response", also led to similar results: 2/3 of patients suffering from high blood pressure showed significant decreases in it after just three months of meditation and, of consequently, they had less need for medicines. This is because relaxation results in the formation of nitric oxide, which opens up blood vessels.

Source: The Journal of Alternative and Complimentary Medicine, NPR News

Transcendental Meditation decreases inflammatory disorders

A study conducted in France and Spain at the UW-Madison Waisman Center indicates that the practice of meditation produces a series of genetic and molecular effects on the participants. More precisely, reduced levels of pro-inflammatory genes were recorded, which then led to a faster recovery of the body from a stressful situation.

Source: University of Winsconsin Madison, & HealthCentral & Medical News Today

Transcendental Meditation decreases inflammation at cellular level

Three studies in which the group that has undertaken the meditation has recorded better results in preventing inflammations at the cellular level than the control groups.

Sources: ScienceDirect (1), ScienceDirect (2), ScienceDirect (3)

Practicing Transcendental Meditation helps prevent asthma, rheumatoid arthritis and inflammatory bowel disease

In a research conducted by a group of neuro-scientists from the University of Wisconsin-Madison, two groups of people have been exposed to different methods of stress control. Some of them received meditation training, while the other group underwent a therapy that included nutrition education, exercise and music. The study concluded that meditation was more effective in alleviating inflammatory symptoms than other well-being activities.

Source: Medical News Today

Transcendental Meditation and meditative prayer help ease the symptoms of menopause and premenstrual syndrome
This is the conclusion of over twenty control studies drawn from PubMed, PsycInfo, and the Cochrane Databases, which involved different meditation techniques, meditative prayer, yoga and relaxation response.

Source: The Journal of Alternative and Complementary Medicine

Transcendental Meditation reduces the risk of contracting Alzheimer's disease and the risk of premature death
The results of a recent research, published online in the journal Brain, Behavior and Immunity, state that only thirty minutes of meditation a day not only reduces the sense of loneliness, but it reduces also the risk of heart disease, depression, Alzheimer's disease and even premature death.

Source: HealthCentral

Learning Transcendental Meditation techniques is useful for patients diagnosed with fibromyalgia
In a study published in PubMed, eleven participants who suffered from fibromyalgia underwent training for eight weeks. As a result, the researchers found a

significant improvement in the participants' general health status and symptoms of stiffness, anxiety and depression. Significant improvements were also observed in the number of days that participants felt good and were not forced to skip work due to fibromyalgia.

Sources: Psychotherapy and Psychosomatics Journal

Transcendental Meditation helps manage heart and respiratory rate

In a study published by the Korean Association of Traditional Genuine Medicine, IAM practitioners, Integrated Amrita Meditation Technique, showed a significant decrease in heart and respiratory rate for up to eight months after the training period.

Source: KoreaScience

Transcendental Meditation can help treating HIV

Quoting a UCLA research, lymphocytes, or simply CD4 T cells, are the "brain" of the immune system, and coordinate their activity when the body is under attack. These are also the cells that are attacked by HIV, the virus that causes AIDS and that has infected about forty million people worldwide. The virus slowly eats CD4 T cells, weakening the immune system.

But the immune system of HIV / AIDS patients must also address another enemy, stress, which can accelerate the decline of CD4 T cells. UCLA researchers report that the practice of meditation is able to stem the decline of CD4 T cells in stressed HIV patients, slowing the progression of the disease.

An eight-week training session focused on stress reduction through meditation was conducted and compared with a one-day monitoring seminar, using a stressed and ethnically diverse sample of forty-eight HIV-positive adults in Los Angeles. Participants in the eight-week group showed no CD4 T-cell loss, indicating that meditation practice was able to stop its decline. In contrast, the control group showed significant decreases in CD4 T cells from the pre-study situation to the post-study situation. Such declines are a feature of HIV progression.

Source: ScienceDaily

Transcendental Meditation can make us live longer
Telomeres are an essential part of human cells that influence their aging process. Although the associated research is not yet conclusive, some data suggest that "some forms of meditation can have healthy effects on

telomere length, reducing cognitive stress and increasing positive moods, hormonal factors that can promote the maintenance of telomeres."

Source: Wiley Online Library

Transcendental Meditation helps manage psoriasis
Psychological stress is a powerful trigger for inflammation. A meditation-based stress reduction intervention administered in an audio cassette during ultraviolet light therapy has helped to stem the lesions of psoriasis patients more quickly.

Sources: NCBI

Transcendental Meditation specific health benefits
As you can see, there is an abundance of studies on the benefits that Transcendental Meditation can bring to our body. Science has proven that this type of meditation is capable of:

Reduce the metabolic syndrome *(Archive of American Medical Association of Internal Medicine)*
Help manage the effects of trauma *(Hindustan Times)*

Extend longevity *(American Journal of Cardiology)*

Reduce blood pressure in teenagers at risk *(American Journal of Hypertension)*

Reduce atherosclerosis *(American Journal of Cardiology)*
Reduce coronary artery thickening *(Stroke)*

Reduce myocardial ischemia *(American Journal of Cardiology)*
Help manage and prevent anxiety *(Psychotherapy and Psychosomatics Journal)*
Help reduce cholesterol *(American Journal of Cardiology,)*
Contribute to the treatment of epilepsy *(Psychotherapy and Psychosomatics Journal)*
Help stop smoking *(Psychotherapy and Psychosomatics Journal)*
Create a state of deep rest in body and mind *(American Journal of Hypertension)*

Increase skin resistance *(Physiology & Behavior)*

Increase the lucidity of thought *(Psychotherapy and Psychosomatics Journal)*
Source: David Lynch Foundation

4. Relationships

Loving kindness meditation improves empathy and relationships

In Buddhist traditions there is a practice called METTA, which we translated as Meditation of loving kindness, in which the practitioner focuses on developing a sense of benevolence and care towards all living beings. According to a study conducted by Emory University, these exercises effectively increase the ability to empathize with others by reading their facial expressions.

Another study points out that the development of positive emotions through compassion causes us to accumulate various personal resources, including "an attitude of love for oneself and one's neighbor, which includes self-acceptance, social support received, and relationships positive with others", as it awakens the "feeling of control over one's life" and includes "paths of thought, environmental mastery, sense of purpose in life, and resilience". Similar results can also be achieved through the practice of TM.

Sources: ScienceDaily

Loving kindness meditation reduces social isolation

In a study published by the American Psychological Association, the subjects who practiced "even a few minutes of this meditation showed a greater sense of social connection and positivity towards others, both at explicit and implicit levels. These results suggest that this easy-to-implement technique can help increase positive social emotions and decrease social isolation". Even in this study Transcendental Meditation has achieved similar results, although of lesser impact.

Source: American Psychological Association

Transcendental Meditation increases our feelings of compassion and reduces worries
After being assigned to nine weeks Cultivation of compassion training (CCT), the individuals undergoing an experiment showed significant improvements in all three areas of compassion - compassion for others, receiving compassion from others, and self-compassion. In a similar situation, practitioners also experienced decreased levels of concern and emotional suppression.

Sources: Stanford School of Medicine

Transcendental Meditation reduces the loneliness feeling
A study conducted by Carnegie Mellon University indicates that Mindfulness is useful in reducing

feelings of loneliness, and consequently mitigates the risk of obesity, mortality and expression of pro-inflammatory genes.

Source: ScienceDirect

Transcendental Meditation reduces the emotional hunger
Scientists believe that Transcendental Meditation helps manage the emotional hunger that causes obesity.

Source: DoctorsOnTM

5. Meditation for kids

As mentioned above, Mindfulness derives directly from TM. As part of a vast collection of studies carried out on meditation in schools, the MindfulnessInSchools.org portal presented the results of research that has scientifically found the following benefits for children who have exercised these practices:

-reduction of depression symptoms

-reduction of somatic stress

-reduced hostility and conflicts with peers

-reduction of anxiety

-reduced reactivity

-reduced drug abuse

-improvement of memory

-more self-care

-greater optimism and positive emotions

-higher self-esteem

-increased feelings of happiness and well-being

-improved social skills

-sleep improvement

-better self-awareness

-better academic performance

There have also been numerous reports of benefits for teachers and school staff assisting, actively participating, including:

-increased personal qualities, as well as greater openness, curiosity, kindness, empathy, compassion, acceptance, trust, patience, and the ability to focus

-improvement of physical and mental health, in particular there was a clear improvement in the conditions particularly relevant for the teaching profession, such as stress and nervous exhaustion

-improved teaching effectiveness

-improved physical health

-increase in the ability to provide more adequate support for students, as a result of being more motivated and autonomous

-stress reductions

-greater work motivation

-improvement of spatial memory, working memory and attention

Source: MindfulnessInSchools.org

6. To conclude, here are some interesting facts about Transcendental Meditation:
-Repeating the mantra "om" before surgery helps in the preparation and post-operative recovery

-Meditators are more able to affect the reality that surrounds us at the quantum level

-Meditation can improve our sex life

-Meditation reduces competitiveness and age bias

Source: Sage Journals

In a nutshell, science confirms the experience of millions of practitioners: Transcendental Meditation helps prevent disease, makes people happier and improves performance in virtually any task, be it physical or mental.

Techniques of Transcendental Meditation

The most useful approach to the practice of Transcendental Meditation is to consider it the most important activity of each day, planning it as if it were an appointment that cannot be missed. The ideal choice is early in the morning, before starting the day's activities. If this is not possible, it is a good rule to choose the best time for your own life and continue regularly. Some find it beneficial to practice twice a day: early in the morning after a restful sleep and in the late afternoon or early evening. However, a dedicated practice is recommended at least once a day.

Finding a place to Meditate
First you need to find a really peaceful place, that is free from intrusions and interruptions by others.

Aspirants to meditation often talk about obstacles created by family and friends. In most cases the fault lies in the aspirant. We talk too much. The way we use those fifteen minutes every morning is only about us, and there is no need to talk about it in the family, or to expect others to be quiet because we want to meditate. If we can't find a time for morning meditation because of family commitments, let's try to find some time later. There is always a way to overcome difficulties, when we are truly committed, a way that does not compromise our decision. As a last resort it is always possible to get up fifteen minutes earlier in the morning.

Position

Once the problem of time and place has been resolved, let's sit comfortably and begin to meditate. Here the question arises: how should we sit? Is the best position crossed-legged, kneeling, sitting, or standing? The best is always the simplest and most natural.

The cross-legged position was, and still is, widely used in the East, and many books have been written on this subject. Some of these positions are connected with the nervous system and with the inner structure of those subtle channels which the Hindus call "nadis", which are subjected to the nervous system recognized in the West.

The negative side of these positions is that they induce two rather undesirable reactions. In the first place they push us to concentrate on the mechanism and not on the purpose of the process and, secondly, they instigate us to frequently try a pleasant sense of superiority, based on the attempt to do something that the majority of people does not and that distinguishes us. In short, we are interested in the formal side of meditation; it deals with the non-self rather than the Self.

We therefore choose the position that most easily allows us to forget the physical body. For Westerners it is probably sitting. It is essential to keep the spine erect; stay relaxed (but not abandoned), so that no part of the body is in a state of tension, with the chin slightly reclined forward, so as to eliminate any stiffness in the back of the neck. Meditation is an inner act, and can only be performed successfully if the body is relaxed, in a balanced position and therefore forgotten.

Breathing
Once obtained a comfortable and relaxed position, and after having diverted the consciousness from the physical body, we turn our attention to the breath, to make sure that it is calm, regular and rhythmic.

At this point, I would like to warn against the use of breathing exercises, unless you have already devoted years to proper meditation and purification of the body. In ancient Eastern teachings, breath control was allowed only after the first three "means of union" (as they are called) were to some extent become part of life, and only by following appropriate instructions.

The practice of breathing exercises has nothing to do with spiritual development. This practice, which is instead connected with psychic development, creates many difficulties and is dangerous. In ancient times, the instructors carefully selected the subjects for this teaching and it was added as a complement to a formation that had already reached a certain degree of contact with the soul, so that it could direct the energies evoked by the breath towards its objectives.

We will therefore limit ourselves to ascertaining that the breath is calm and regular and we will completely withdraw the thoughts from the body to begin concentration.

Visualization and Creative use of Imagination
The next step in the practice of Transcendental Meditation is the use of imagination; we represent the triple lower man aligned or in direct communication with the soul. It is possible to do it in many ways. This is what is called visualization. One could say that visualization, imagination and will are the three most important factors in any creative process. They are the subjective causes of many objective effects.

At the beginning, visualization is above all a matter of experimental faith. We know that, through reasoning, we have come to understand that within and beyond all manifested things there exists an Ideal Model that seeks to manifest itself on the physical plane. The use of visualization, imagination and will is part of the activities planned to accelerate the emergence of that Ideal.

When we visualize we use our highest conception of that ideal, covered with some kind of matter, usually mental, not yet being able to conceive higher forms or types of substance with which to wrap our images.

When we form a mental image, the substance of our mind vibrates at a certain frequency and attracts a corresponding type of mental substance in which the mind is immersed. Will keeps the image still and gives it life. This process takes place whether or not we are able to see it in the mind's eye. If we do not see it, it does not matter, as the creative work proceeds equally. Perhaps one day we will learn how to follow and consciously implement the whole process.

With regard to this work, sometimes in the initial phase the beginner represents the three bodies (the three aspects of formal nature) connected by a shining body of light, or visualizes three centers of vibrating energy, stimulated by a higher and more powerful center; others imagine the soul as a triangle of strength, to which the triangle of lower nature is connected by the silver thread that the Bible talks about, the sutratma, or thread of the soul of the Eastern Scriptures, or the life line of others schools of thought. Still others prefer to stick to the concept of a unified personality, connected to the immanent Divinity: the Christ in us, hope of glory.

The choice of the image to be used has little importance, as long as we start from the basic idea of the Self that seeks contact with the not-self, its instrument in the worlds of human expression and, vice versa, from the concept of non-self pushed to turn to its source of life. Once this is achieved, we can continue the meditation. The physical and emotional bodies fall, in turn, below the threshold of consciousness, we concentrate in the mind and try to bend it to our will.

From what we have said so far, the need for a Master is quite evident, that is a guide who knows how to accompany us to move correctly the first steps towards the practice of Transcendental Meditation.

Concentration

It is precisely at this point that our problem arises. The mind refuses to adhere to the thoughts we want to formulate and struggles in all directions in its usual search for subjects. We cannot concentrate on the thought itself and we think instead about what we will do later, about someone we have to talk to, or about a project that is close to our heart; we begin to think of a person we love and immediately fall back into the world of emotions and we have to start all over again.

Then we gather our thoughts and start again with good success for half a minute, then we remember a commitment that we have taken or a job that we have to do and we find ourselves again in the field of mental reactions forgetting the line of thought we intended to follow. Once again we gather our scattered ideas and resume the work of taming the rebellious mind. Only with constant practice we will finally be able to maintain mental concentration with a certain degree of effectiveness.

How to reach this condition? Following a formula or a pattern of meditation that automatically establishes an insurmountable limit to the mind and tells it: "you can go there and no further". Carefully and thoughtfully we establish precise boundaries to mental activity, so that it is possible to see immediately when we cross them. We then know that we must withdraw ourselves again within the shelters that we ourselves have built.

The sincere investigator will try to start a form of meditation to help develop concentration.

In conclusion, these are the Stages of Transcendental Meditation:

1) Take a comfortable position that allows you to control your body.
2) Make sure the breath is rhythmic and regular.

155

3) Visualize the triple lower self (physical, emotional and mental): a) in contact with the soul; b) as a channel for soul energy directed to the brain through the mind. Now the physical apparatus can be controlled by the soul.

4) Focus precisely by appealing to the will. This means striving to keep the mind fixed on certain words, so that their meaning is clear in our mind and not just the words themselves, or the fact that we are trying to meditate.

5) Repeat your Mantra with concentrated attention. An example of Mantra is: "More radiant than the sun, purer than snow, more subtler than ether is the Self, the Spirit that is in me. I am that Self. That Self is me."

6) Do not allow the mind to relax its concentration on the meaning, content or implications of the repeated Mantra.

7) Conclude intentionally the concentration work.

This is certainly a meditation for beginners. It contains some important points through which a thought gathering process is carried out and a refocusing method is used.

Transcendental Meditation as a lifestyle

It is advisable to reserve a certain amount of time each day for this particular job. At the beginning, fifteen minutes are more than enough. We must be sincere with ourselves and see things for what they are. The excuse "I have no time" is really silly and it only denotes lack of interest. If someone says they can't find fifteen minutes out of the one thousand four hundred and forty that make up the day, isn't it fair to say that what they really lack is interest?

First of all, we will try to find time to meditate early in the morning. This is the most suitable moment because, after having participated in the daily events and the alternate exchanges of life, the mind is in a state of violent vibration; this is not the case if meditation is done first thing in the morning. The mind is then relatively calm and can be quickly tuned with the higher states of consciousness.

Moreover, if we begin the day by focusing our attention on the spiritual aspects and activities of the soul, we will live that day in a different way. If this becomes a habit, we will soon notice a change in our reactions to life events, and we will also notice that we are beginning to formulate the thoughts that the soul

157

thinks. Thus begins the operating process of a law, since "as a man thinks, such he is".

It is evident, therefore, that the man who learns to meditate must try to do two things.

First. He must learn to "introduce" into his mind and then correctly interpret what he has seen and perceived, to transmit it accurately and accurately to the impressionable and attentive brain.

Second. He must learn to know the nature of the energies contacted and practice using them properly. Here is a practical example that everyone knows. We are moved by anger or irritation. We instinctively raise our voices. Why? Emotional energy dominates us. By learning to control the energy of verbal expression, we begin to dominate that particular type of emotional energy.

In these two concepts, correct interpretation, transmission and the right use of energy, all the essence of Transcendental Meditation is summed up. It also appears evident what the student's problem is and why every wise meditation instructor insists with his students on the need to use prudence and to proceed step by step.

Need for Common sense

The dangers of meditation are largely inherent in our own virtues, and here lies much of the difficulty. They are, to a large extent, the dangers of a high mental conception that anticipates the capacity of the lower vehicles, especially the dense physical one. The absolute necessity, for the student of occultism, is to consider a strong common sense as one of its basic qualities, not separated from a happy sense of proportions that induces, due caution and the approximation of the method necessary, to the immediate need. Therefore, to those who wish to undertake the process of occult meditation, I say:

-Know yourself;
-Proceed slowly and carefully;
-Study the effects;
-Cultivate the realization that eternity is long and that what is slowly built lasts forever;
-Aspire to regularity;
-Always understand that true spiritual effects must be noted in the esoteric life of service;
-Also remember that psychic phenomena are not a sign of success in the practice of meditation.

The world will see the effects, and it will be the best judge of the same practitioner. But, above all, the Master will know them, since the results on the causal levels will appear to Him long before the student himself is aware of any progress.

51903482R00097

Made in the USA
San Bernardino, CA
04 September 2019